Build $1,000,000 Net Worth

While Achieving Perfect Credit

Jeffrey M. Fazio, M.Ed.

Jeff Fazio Books

Build Million-Dollar Net Worth: While Achieving Perfect Credit

Copyright © 2018 by Jeffrey M. Fazio, M.Ed.

All rights reserved. No part of this book may be used or reproduced in any manner whatsoever without written permission except in the case of brief quotations embodied in critical articles and reviews.

Editing by Susan Miers Smith
For information: jmf191@gmail.com

FIRST EDITION

ISBN 978-1985674554

Cover design by Jeffrey M. Fazio.

*Dedicated to my loving wife, Terry-Ann,
who inspired, motivated, and gently harassed me to write this.*

"A fool and his money are soon parted."

—Thomas Tusser

CONTENTS

Chapter 1	$20,000 Cell Phone	*Page 1*

Three Pillars of Financial Health

Chapter 2:	Net Worth: A Measure of Financial Value	*Page 5*
Chapter 3:	Credit Score: A Measure of Credit Worthiness	*Page 13*
Chapter 4:	Income: A Measure of Financial Productivity	*Page 23*

Large Expenses

Chapter 5	Housing: Living Below Your Means	*Page 41*
Chapter 6	Automobiles: A Losing Purchase	*Page 53*
Chapter 7	Taxes: An Optional Expense	*Page 61*
Chapter 8	Shopping: Managing to Save Money	*Page 67*
Chapter 9	Traveling: It Doesn't Have to be Expensive	*Page 81*
Chapter 10	Negotiating: Know the Value	*Page 95*

Habits

Chapter 11	Bad Habits: Choices that Cost	*Page 107*
Chapter 12	Good Habits: Choices that Pay	*Page 131*

Example

Chapter 13	Buying Your Preferred Home for Free	*Page 143*
Chapter 14	Comparing $50K Salaries	*Page 149*

Conclusion

Chapter 15	Money: How to Spend It	*Page 159*

Preface

On some level, I suppose, I am not really qualified to write a book on personal finances.

I do not have advanced degrees in economics, nor have I accumulated a million dollars. No major companies, or even minor ones for that matter, list me as their CEO. My day job has nothing to do with managing a large investment portfolio. I have not done miraculous things with a large inheritance or sudden lottery winning.

I was, however, bankrupt the month before I turned 25.

That was something.

Now, a couple of decades later, I have an almost perfect credit score, haven't paid a dime in credit card interest in more than 15 years, and I am well on my way to creating a million-dollar net worth. My highest recorded credit score was 846 — just shy of a perfect 850.

I have learned some very simple, but important, financial lessons along the way. There is no magic to be learned here. The reader looking for the get rich quick scheme has found the wrong book.

This book is for marathoners, not sprinters.

In fact, this book isn't even about getting rich. It is about building wealth and credit. The finances of the rich may rest on the whim of an employer or the "market" (whatever that means). I have seen colleagues with incredibly high salaries flounder when they lose their positions. I have seen rich people that can't make their mortgage payments.

Properly built wealth is more solid — more stable. Those with wealth and credit can weather a variety of financial storms.

This book isn't geared toward the wealthy or the rich. It is geared toward you, the typical reader looking to improve the hand you were dealt. As my friend David would say, it is for the person who is looking to "increase their luck" although I would suggest nothing I have done or I am writing about has to do with actual luck.

Studies have shown that there is a positive correlation between salaries and happiness. It turns out that the more you make the happier you really are more likely to be. The plot twist is that this correlation only lasts up to roughly $70,000/year in salary.

Once you are comfortably meeting basic life needs (food, shelter, etc.), there is not any more significant increase in happiness with additional increases in salary (I'm still more than willing to accept a higher salary to contribute to this data).

That said, this book is written for those in mind that are employed, but not making $70,000 per year or more. This book will be most beneficial to those making under $60,000 per year and are in the 20-35 year old range. If you are making over $60,000 per year and are struggling with debt or have not attained significant assets, this book is also for you. Regardless of your exact situation, I am sure there will be nuggets of wisdom in here that could apply to anyone.

I have no doubt that I will reach my financial goals of a perfect 850 credit score and a million dollar net worth.

Won't you join me?

Chapter 1

$20,000 Cell Phone

One night in December of 2002, I was hanging out with one of my best friends, Joey Branford. We were talking about his friend Chris Rado. The previous night, Rado had a $20,000 Vertu cell phone stolen at a nightclub in Orlando, Florida.

It's hard to imagine a cell phone worth $20,000 now, much less back in 2002 before smart phones existed. What makes a cell phone worth that much money? It was a platinum phone, with a sapphire faceplate and ruby buttons. It featured a carrying case made of the same leather they use in the interiors of Rolls Royces and a special button that accessed a 24-hour concierge. The phone also boasted coverage in the U.S., Europe and Asia.

We knew Chris had access to money — lots of money. It was no secret that he and his family were wealthy, but it was still hard to imagine a cell phone of that value. As the conversation progressed, Joey made the comment that if either of us added up everything we owned we wouldn't have $20,000 worth of value. I laughed with him, but in my mind I figured he must be wrong — at least on my end.

After Joey left, I took stock of my life. In a few weeks I was going to be 29 years old. I was just entering my third year as a graphic designer and photographer for a large city newspaper and I had a side hustle waiting tables in a fine-dining restaurant. I was making just over $40,000/year, had a modest (*ok, slight*) 401(k) retirement plan, and was feeling pretty good that I was actually utilizing a Bachelor of Fine Arts degree.

At the time I was living in a small apartment, modernly furnished, and I owned 4 vehicles that were all bought with cash. I also had a pile of camera equipment. Surely I had $20,000 worth of "stuff."

I didn't.

How was this possible? I had been working since I was 15 years old and in those 13 years of employment I recorded over $275,000 in income with Uncle Sam. Certainly I had managed to convert some of that income into assets that had value. Was it really possible that I hadn't transformed even 7% of my earning into tangible, retained value?

It was.

As I took account of my assets, I owned two 1991 Toyota MR2s. They were bought used for $1750 and $5,500. I also had a 1998 Toyota MR2 that was purchased for $1,500. The fourth vehicle in my stable was a 1987 Chevy Sprint which was also acquired for a mere $1,500. That is four vehicles, bought used, for a total of $10,250.

Although the photography equipment was professional grade, it was getting older and obsolete as it was film-based. The digital revolution in cameras had taken over and I hadn't bothered to keep up since I had access to all the cool camera equipment at the newspaper.

The apartment was modernly furnished, but was done 90% through inexpensive Ikea furniture and 10% from revitalizing thrift store finds (*using that fine arts background again*). There simply wasn't much value there.

With cars, furniture, and cameras not eclipsing $15,000 in value, it was becoming apparent that the $20K figure Joey mentioned us not achieving might be true.

There was no money invested in the stocks or bonds. My name was not on any real estate deeds. Any jewelry or art objects I possessed were of inconsequential value.

The only gold I owned was a 14kt rope bracelet and matching necklace left over of from the early '90s. I had never collected stamps and the only thing left from my childhood foray into coin collecting were proof sets from 1973 and the 1976 Bicentennial.

I didn't even have a saving's account.

I had one more card up my sleeve — that corporate-backed 401(k) retirement plan. Surely that would be enough to push me over the value of a friend's friend's cell phone.

As mentioned, I was only two years into the newspaper career and the 401(k) benefit was not worth bragging about — even with my contributions. With only a few thousand dollars in that account, it wasn't going to be enough to eclipse $20,000.

There I sat, alone in my apartment, on the cusp of my 29th birthday, accepting the reality that I managed to *not* accumulate $20,000 worth of "stuff" in my life thus far.

Chapter 2

Net Worth: A Measure of Financial Value
Three Pillars of Financial Health

The really unfortunate part of this story, looking back, isn't that I hadn't accrued $20,000 of assets in my life. It was that I failed to even consider the implications to my actual worth — *my net worth*.

What is net worth? Net worth is a measure of your financial health. It is a simple measurement really. All that is required is to add up the value of all of the assets you possess and subtract the total of all of your liabilities (debts).

If everything you own is worth $50,000 and you have $30,000 of debt, then your net worth is $20,000.

Consequently, if your assets add up to $30,000 and your debts total $50,000, your net worth is *negative* $20,000. Imagine that — having a negative value.

That was my reality back in December of 2002. Although I carried no credit card debt and I paid cash for all of my vehicles, I had well over $40,000 in student loans for my undergraduate degree and I had just signed up for a grad program which would eventually add another $20,000 to that sum. I was deep into negative territory.

Most people do not talk about, much less consciously think about, their net worth. Not surprisingly, many people have a negative net worth. Although they are not talking or thinking about it, it is often something one intuitively feels and it doesn't feel good. It's no wonder that many people are depressed and many couples argue about finances.

My wife and I are very happy people and we have never had a single argument or concern about finances. We are not infinitely wealthy, nor do we have jobs that pay incredibly high salaries.

What we do have, is a strong sense of our worth — *our net worth*. In fact, we calculate it every single month. It is a habit I started in November of 2011 — 9 years after realizing I didn't own $20,000 of assets.

$$

In November of 2011 I was four months into a new job. Although the new job had a healthy salary increase, it also substantially increased my daily commute from 5 minutes to an hour. I wanted to find a solution to this dilemma that not only saved me time, but also money. Wouldn't it be even better if I could craft a solution that made me money and increased my assets?

Throughout 2011 I had been reading a lot of books on investing, and I made several important financial decisions at this point that would change my life. As I was planning to move, I decided to rent out my home instead of selling it.

A few months earlier, I had also taken out a second mortgage, at a low interest rate, on that home so that I would have a down payment on an investment property.

In the few years before this move, the housing bubble burst and the laws changed to inhibit home buyers from borrowing money to use as a down payment. This type of behavior was frowned upon as it was one of the contributing factors to many people getting in over-their-heads with multiple mortgages and not having any equity in the property.

Generally speaking, when you apply for a new mortgage they look back over your last six months of transactions. The cash I received from the second mortgage I had put into the stock market in what I felt to be reasonably safe stocks. I moved the money around cautiously in the market over the next few months while I looked for the right investment property.

My goal was to find a two- or three-unit apartment building with the intention of living in one unit and having the other unit(s) pay for the building.

$$

Having done a lot of reading on investing, and now possessing a solid plan and knowing my goals, it was time to regularly monitor my net worth — my financial health. Just like we monitor our physical health, I intended to keep an eye on the pulse of my financial life.

I scoured the internet for Excel-based net worth calculators. There are many out there and all of the ones I found were designed to be a snap shot of your net worth. You simply entered everything you owned in the assets column and everything you owed in the debts column. Voila! It calculated your net worth.

This was helpful, but I did not want to capture a momentary glimpse of my blood pressure. I wanted a tool that would consistently monitor my heart rate.

I found the best net worth calculator I could and I modified it so that it could be used over time to accurately graph my financial health on a monthly basis.

$$

December 1, 2011 was the first time I entered numbers into my new tool — *my net worth calculator*. As I entered my end-of-the-month numbers for November, I was pleased, but not surprised to see a positive number even though I now had nearly $60,000 in student loan debt. At that moment, my net worth was $50,154.

Obviously I had made some changes in my financial life between 2002 and 2011 to go from a negative net worth to a clearly positive value. Seeing proof that my life changes had such a positive effect on my financial health was incredibly rewarding.

Ever since that date, I have religiously entered my month-end-numbers into that Excel spreadsheet. It has truly changed my life and has drastically changed my net worth (as of June 2016 my personal net worth was $153,543).

I would estimate that after my first 13 years of work, my net worth was negative $35,000. In the next nine years of work it increased to $50,000 and the next 4.5 years it jumped over $100,000 more. Technically, those 4.5 years only included four years of actual work as I had taken off the last six months of 2015.

$$

How was I able to increase net worth so quickly in the later years? It is true that I moved up in positions and salary; however, I know many people that make more money and get further into debt resulting in a significant loss of net worth. How many people, upon receiving a promotion or better position, look to buy a new car or more expensive home?

The simple truth is my net worth has gone up quicker and quicker for the exact same reason that runners see lower and lower blood pressure and bodybuilders lose more fat and gain more muscle. There was a significant change in my focus and I checked my personal habits to keep on task with my goals.

Gym rats weigh themselves. Runners can monitor their blood pressure. I check-in monthly with a net worth calculator.

I'm a numbers person and I am a competitive person. Measure something about me and I will take it as a challenge to improve it. All I needed was to make that first check of my net worth.

At this point, you might be imaging a lifestyle of ramen noodles, buying second-hand clothes, and no social life. The reality is quite opposite. In the last few years I have eaten better, traveled more, and enjoyed a more fulfilling social life. It is true I watch my spending more and I have found a lot of interesting ways to spend better, but we will get to that in later chapters.

When you monitor your net worth, it becomes apparent that there are two sides of the equation — assets and liabilities. Dieters often make the mistake of waiting to see gains simply by eating less, but they ignore the second side of that equation. You will only get so far with lowering calories. To see significant gains, proper exercise will accentuate burning calories.

That said, you will only get so far reducing debts and spending. If you really want to make significant gains, you need to increase your assets — real assets.

If you are renting, look at buying. If you are looking at buying, look at investing in a property with income potential. Real estate can be one the best investments you can make. Always look for ways to make a better deal for you, for the long haul.

Educate yourself on investment options (stocks, bonds, mutual funds, and certificates of deposit - CDs). These tools can be boring and uninteresting to read about, but they are lessons for a lifetime and will help you start to build a solid financial portfolio.

I would be remiss to not address the liability side of the equation. When I started my financial planning, I had the advantage of having no credit card debt. If you are carrying credit card debt — any credit card debt — I strongly encourage you to make it a priority in your life to eliminate *that* debt. Credit card debt is financial quick sand.

When you are signing onto any new debt (car loans, personal loans, student loans, mortgages, credit cards, etc.) make sure you understand the terms and any potential paths for eliminating that debt sooner than the full term. Not all debt is bad and we will discuss that later. In fact, there are some really great reasons to take on debt and it can drastically help your net worth.

$$

My net worth from June of 2016 will be the last personal value I am sharing as I was married in July of 2016. Marriage will always have an impact on your assets and liabilities. That said, my net worth is no longer my focus as my wife and I are now interested in *our net worth*. We're a team and she is now just as excited to watch our worth grow as I am.

When we first met, she was not actively monitoring her net worth to the degree that I had been, but she was very diligent about her finances. She wasn't carrying unnecessary debt and was invested in her own real estate.

$$

So, what are you worth? Without calculating it, do you have an idea if your net worth is positive or negative? If so, do you know how far in either direction?

I assure you, checking your worth on a monthly basis will affect how you see money, your purchases, and all other financial decisions. Let's be honest, you are more likely to lose weight if you stand on a scale regularly. It's time to step up!

Chapter 3

Credit Scores: A Measure of Credit Worthiness
Three Pillars of Financial Health

Numbers. Numbers. Numbers. So much of life is about numbers. This is especially true in the financial world.

Your credit score is another significant number in your financial health check-up list. What is your credit score? This number identifies how well you manage credit. The scores are 3-digit numbers that fall on a range from 300 up to 850.

Your credit score is also called a FICO score. It was designed by the Fair Isaac Corporation. On the credit scale, any score below 580 is considered very poor credit. 580 up to 669 is fair credit. Good credit covers 670 through 739. A score of 740 to 799 is very good credit. Exceptional credit starts at 800 and ends with a perfect score of 850.

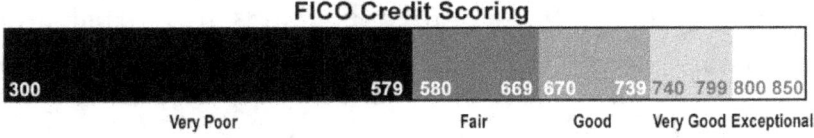

Who is responsible for calculating your score? There are three major credit bureaus that receive all sorts of information on your financial transactions involving debt and credit. The three bureaus are TransUnion, Experian, and Equifax.

Technically, they use their own calculations called the VantageScore, but it lands on the same 300–850 range. The breakdown of good versus bad credit falls within similar ranges.

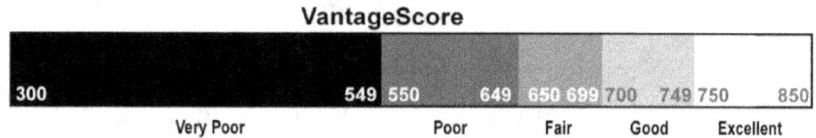

$$

Why care about your credit score? The reality is credit scores have a lot of influence in our lives. Lenders use these numbers as part of the decision-making process when you apply for loans and credit. That said, every time you fill out a credit card application, mortgage or car loan, someone is looking up your credit score.

Not only is this number used to determine if they will extend you the credit requested, but it will also be used to determine the terms of the offer. Even if your credit is good enough to get the loan, you might not get the best possible interest rate. It could also affect the amount of money that is required for a down payment.

Let's look at an example to see what bad credit could really cost you.

Person A: They have great credit and are buying a house for $100,000. They are putting down $20,000 so they need a mortgage for $80,000. They take out a typical 30-year mortgage and are offered an interest rate of 4%. Since they are putting 20% down, they are not required to purchase Private Mortgage Insurance (PMI).

Their monthly mortgage payment for principal (the amount borrowed) and interest (the fee paid to the bank for borrowing the money) would be $381.93. Over the course of their loan, they will pay $57,495.61 in interest.

Person B: Their credit is not as good and they do not have as much money saved for a down payment. They only have $9,000 to put down. They apply for the same mortgage as Person A, but the bank will only approve them for a 6% mortgage and they are requiring them to put down 10%.

Since they do not have 10%, $10,000, they can't buy the $100K property. They need to look for a $90,000 property which they find and settle on.

They now have a mortgage for $81,000 for 30 years at 6% interest. Since they did not have 20% down, they also have to pay 1% in PMI. The PMI must be paid until they get to 20% equity in the home.

Their monthly mortgage payment for principal and interest would be $553.14. Once they make 88 payments (just over 7 years) they will have 20% equity, but to remove the PMI from their payment, they will have to pay several hundred dollars to have the house appraised again to ensure the property has not lost value.

If they are able to remove the PMI, their monthly payments drop to $485.64 for the remainder of the loan.

Over the course of their entire mortgage, they will pay $87,888.93 in interest. Person B ends up paying more in interest than the total amount of the principal!

Comparison: Person A purchased a *more* valuable house and had monthly payments that were $171.21 *less* than Person B. Over the course of the loans, Person B paid

$30,393.32 *more* in interest. Person B also had to pay a few hundred extra dollars for the appraisal to remove the PMI.

I think it is clear that life is much better for Person A. This interest math works the same, albeit on a smaller scale, for car loans and credit cards. It literally pays to have good credit.

$$

As you are getting to know me, it should be no surprise that I monitor my credit score closely. In fact, I check it twice per month with two of the three credit bureaus.

In the past you had to pay to see your actual credit score. Now, many lenders offer this service for free. One of my credit cards updates me once per month with my TransUnion score and one of the banks I deal with does the same with my Experian score.

A perfect credit score is one of my financial goals. My highest recorded score so far has been 846 with TransUnion. I'm almost there. I have no doubt that I will get there.

This was not always the case for me. When I was younger I did not understand credit and I failed completely at managing it. A few months shy of my 25th birthday I was bankrupt. My income was low and I had tens of thousands of dollars in credit card debt, car loans, and personal loans. I filed for bankruptcy and my credit score, that I was not paying attention to anyway, dropped to 460.

That was 1998. Since then, I have not paid a penny in credit card interest. I learned a valuable lesson and turned my life, and credit score, around.

$$

What all goes into your credit score and how can you improve it?

A lot of different things will affect your credit score and all of it comes from your credit report. One of the big factors is your payment history on loans and credit cards. Late payments will negatively affect your credit score.

The number of credit accounts you have, the length of time you have had them, and the types of credit all factor in to the score.

Your total debt influences the score as does your Credit Utilization Rate. The Credit Utilization Rate is a number that indicates how much of your revolving credit (like credit cards) is being used when the score is calculated. If you are carrying high balances on your credits cards and are close to your limits, your credit is going to be negatively affected.

Public records also impact your score. This includes bankruptcy, civil judgments, or tax liens.

If you open up a lot of new credit accounts in a short amount of time, that will also ding your score. In fact, inquiries of your credit report will also impact your score.

If you are shopping for a loan and have a number of banks accessing your credit report you may see a decline in your score.

Now that you see what goes into your credit score, you may start to realize what it takes to build good credit—or truly excellent credit.

Let me tell you the strategies that I have used to bounce back from a 460 up to an 846 score.

Unlike when I was screwing up my twenties, I now carry very few credit cards. I have one major store credit card that I only use once or twice per year. Store credit cards give diversity to your report over the major credit cards and it has allowed me to grow a long history—remember, length of open accounts is a good thing if the credit is used responsibly.

I also have major credit cards with Discover and VISA. I'll get into more details about credit cards in a later chapter. For now, know that for most transactions in my life, I was using the Discover card. I really only had the Visa for the random places that do not accept Discover and for having another open line of credit.

That's it. I had only 3 major credit cards for a very long time. Only recently have I opened a new Visa card and I only did that because I moved outside of the U.S. The country I am living in currently does not widely accept Discover and the Visa card I had been using for years is problematic outside of the U.S. It was just easier to open a new account with a bank that worked better for living outside the country.

For credit diversity, which helps your credit score, I do maintain one national store credit card with JC Penney. I use it once or twice per year and only to keep the account active. Having a variety of credit increases your score.

I charge most things I purchase and I pay my credit card off, in full, every month. Not only do I pay it off in full, but I also pay it off well before the due date. In fact, I know my Discover statement usually comes into my in-box on the 23rd of the month. There have been many times that I have logged into my Discover account on the 22nd or early on the 23rd and seen that my statement was ready. When that happens, I simply pay the bill immediately. It is rewarding getting the confirmation email that I paid my bill a few hours before they even sent it!

As I have responsibly used credit for a very long time now, my card limits are rather high which also helps my score as I do not maintain a balance. I am showing the credit scorers that they can trust me with credit.

Another strategy that I employ is in regards to my mortgages. I also pay them immediately on the bill date (not the due date!). I also overpay the mortgage(s) every month, even if it is only a few dollars. Not only am I showing responsibility with the loan, but I am paying it off faster and saving a lot of money in interest over the life of the loan (more on that later).

As a general rule, I do not do car loans or personal loans. If I need cash, I prefer to do a 2nd mortgage or home equity line of credit. They tend to have better interest rates and the interest you pay is often tax deductible.

Years of monitoring my credit score and paying attention to my payments has resulted in my near perfect credit score. My credit responsibility is now habit so I am sure that in time, that perfect score will come.

Incidentally, another reason to monitor your credit score regularly is it can alert you to fraudulent activity happening under your name. This is a very real concern and having any indicators that something is awry with your good name and credit is important. The credit companies are also much easier to work with the earlier you catch fraud.

Chapter 4

Income: A Measure of Financial Productivity
Three Pillars of Financial Health

Income is the third pillar that holds up the status of your financial well-being. The three pillars are net worth, credit score, and income.

Your income is a measure of how financially productive you are. How much monetary value you do you produce?

Net worth tells you how much of that cash value you are retaining. Sometimes it is not how much, you make, but rather how much you keep.

The credit score indicates how well you manage debt. Are you smart with money and managing debt well?

When you have a reasonably decent income, have good credit, and are regularly seeing increases in your net worth, it has a lot of positive effects on your life. We already addressed two of the pillars. Let's discuss income.

Please do not confuse income with salary. If you ask most people, "How much do you make?" Their thoughts immediately go to their hourly rate of pay or their salary. Most people identify their earnings with their paycheck which is natural to do since it is often the first, and probably largest, place the average person has income.

If you have a basic savings account, it is probably earning interest from the bank. That is also income. Chances are the amount of money coming from that interest might be insignificant unless you happen to have a very significant amount of money in the bank, but that money is still income.

Maybe you have some money invested directly in stocks that pay a dividend — that is income. Do you have a retirement plan through your employer? It is possible that some of those investments are earning dividends. If you are not following your retirement accounts, you might have money coming in that you are not aware of. Granted, most of those accounts are setup as Dividend Re-Investment Programs (DRIPs) so you do not directly receive the cash from the dividends. It gets reinvested into more shares which means, through compounding, that the wealth builds.

Do you have anything in place which earns money while you are working? Maybe you sell stuff online, have an ad-revenue generating YouTube channel, or rent out a spare bedroom. These are all income.

It is time to start thinking about income differently.

$$

If you want to build wealth and your net worth, it will happen more quickly with multiple streams of income. There is a terrific book, *Cashflow Quadrant*, which goes into this subject much deeper than will happen here.

The full title of the book is *Cashflow Quadrant: Guide to Financial Freedom* and is written by Robert Kiyosaki. Mr.

Kiyosaki is the author of the *Rich Dad, Poor Dad* series of books. I have read several of his books and they are all a good starting point for reading about managing your financial life.

The basic premise of *Cashflow Quadrant* is there are 4 areas in our life where we produce income: employment, investment, business ownership, and self-employment. Most people are only finding income in the first quadrant as an employee.

Mr. Kiyosaki's books inspired me in a number of ways and really challenged me to start developing multiple income streams.

$$

If you maintain your employment as your only source of income, you can still build your net worth with many of the suggestions in this book. It will just be a slower process, unless you are fortunate enough to have a fat pay check.

I can't tell you what additional income streams will work for you, but I am willing to share some of my personal experiences that have inspired me to keep finding other ways to develop cash flow.

$$

From 2002 through 2006, I was building and racing a car on weekends. This was during the time that I was working for the newspaper as a graphic artist and photographer.

Racing cars can get quite expensive and early on I needed to find ways to support my interest. I began negotiating sponsorship deals for both advertising on my car and on the Website I created for documenting my racing adventures. I will not go into detail here on the creativity I used in ascertaining sponsorship, but if you are curious, you can check out my other book *Sponsorship: Amateur Motorsports*.

As soon as I was able to develop income, even a small amount, from sponsorship, I formalized what I was doing as a business venture: Jekyl Hyde Racing. If you are curious, you can check out the Website here: www.JekylHydeRacing.com

Besides the ability to bring in money into my racing activities, there was also an immediate tax benefit from doing this. Suddenly everything I was paying to build my car and race it became a giant tax deduction. The interesting thing with businesses is that tax deductions can be taken even if you are not successful.

I'm not a tax account, so I encourage you to work with your accountant on endeavors you may make and to understand current laws. When I started my racing business, the IRS allowed you up to 3 tax years to *not* make a profit and claim deductions. They figure if you are going into a 4th year of losing money it must be a hobby—not a business.

With the amount I was spending on racing (entry fees, travel, parts, mechanics, etc.), my losses created a substantial tax break. Interestingly, the racing also benefited because this freed up more cash to invest and brought in more sponsorship. In fact, over the course of the next few years, I was doing much better as a "business" and bringing in income.

If you are working on something on the side, even if you are just knees-deep into your favorite hobby, look for ways to formalize it as a business. There may be terrific tax advantages and, if you are fortunate enough, your "business" might just take off.

At the time that I was racing cars, my girlfriend was a full-time jeweler working for a large department store chain. On weekends, she was also making her own personal jewelry and selling it at craft shows. Not surprisingly, she formalized it as a business and was able to start documenting her income and deducting any losses.

Having seen this process, both through my racing and her jewelry, I would strongly encourage you to make your largest purchases (investments) in your business in those first 3 years to maximize potential deductions.

$$

As I got more involved with my racing, I accrued a lot of racing footage. I decided to make a DVD of my racing adventures for myself. I was pretty happy with what I created so I decided to package it and offer it for sale.

Through online message boards I had small following of fans that kept up with my racing so I figured I could sell a few DVDs. I'll never forget putting the DVDs for sale online on a Sunday night, going to bed, getting up to go to work on Monday, and coming home to see that I had sold enough DVDs to profit a little over a $100.

Realizing that I had earned additional income *while I was at work* was a very significant moment for me. It really underscored the power of multiple lines of income working at the same time. The internet was literally making me money while I was off doing something else.

The same was true the following weekend while I was off on another racing endeavor. I was away racing, but the internet was still selling my DVDs. I still had money coming in.

I'm no longer selling DVDs, but I do have a couple of books for sale on Amazon: this book, the one on garnering racing sponsorship, and one on a different personal quest of mine: to run a 5K in all 50 states in 1 year.

Although I am not getting rich on book sales (maybe I will someday), it is terrific to get some additional monthly income for the rest of my life on the efforts I already expended.

$$

Although I did well enough with racing sponsorship to keep improving the car and entering events, it was never going to be something that brought in positive cash flow. Realizing that, and the fact that I had accomplished all of my goals in racing, I decided it was time to cash out—and cash out I did.

When I decided to close Jekyl Hyde Racing, I had acquired many assets (two races cars, a truck, a 20' enclosed trailer, and all sorts of equipment and tools).

These all had real, cash value and this is where Jekyl Hyde Racing finally made a positive impact to my bank account.

When everything was sold and all of the receipts were accounted for, I had walked away with over $36,000. I was extremely fortunate to leave racing with that level of cash and having enjoyed 4 years of a variety racing activities.

$$

Having that kind of cash, I needed to make some decisions on where to move that money. I made a few purchases that included two cars. When those transactions were complete, I still had just over $10,000 and I did not want it to simply sit in a savings account making minimal interest. I wanted to put that money to work for me and the stock market seemed like a fine idea.

During my mid-twenties, I dabbled in the U.S. stock exchange and made a little money and lost a little more. It was never significant enough to convince me that it was a good idea.

In 2001 the "dot com" bubble burst and the little bit I had in the market took a hit. At the time, I was messing around with low value stocks and, even a few penny stocks (penny stocks are those valued under $5 per share). Stocks under $5 per share tend to be very speculative and my *gambling* in the market did not pay off. It was enough to spook me out of the market for a number of years.

I italicized gambling in the preceding paragraph as I was putting money into the market with very little knowledge, insight, or experience. I was truly hoping to buy a bunch of low value stocks and see them take off suddenly making me a pile of money. It rarely works out that way and almost never for someone who has not done at least some level of research into which stocks are being bought.

When you play in the market like I was doing, you are gambling. You might as well buy lottery tickets.

It wasn't until years later, when I cashed out of racing, that I took a more pragmatic and informed approach to the stock market. I had $10,000 to invest and I wanted to see my money work for me.

Instead of gambling, I started swing trading. Swing trading is buying and selling stocks on news that will positively or negatively affect the price. It requires paying more attention to the market and the news, but you can make some money doing it.

I developed a more conservative approach to choosing stocks after reading books and articles geared toward the market. No longer was my money going into small, unheard of companies. I was putting my money into large, developed corporations that paid quarterly dividends.

I would trade on small swings, just looking for a 1-2% increase in value. I was not looking for the "big score" anymore. I was *making money* in the market and it was paying off.

My feeling was that if I got caught on a bad swing in my trading, I would still own a valuable company that would send me dividend checks every 3 months. It felt as though it had much lower risk and I did very well doing this.

Between 2009 and 2013, I made over $19,000 in the market through swing trades and dividends. In my highest year I cleared $9,000 and in my lowest year only $1,200. Overall, I would say I did well swing trading up until 2014.

In 2014 I learned a very hard lesson about the stock market and the U.S. tax laws. I was over $6,000 up in the market that year and on my way for my second best year of trading when the market tanked.

My plan was well in place for this type of experience — even as bad as the crash was. I was holding almost all of my money in The Coca-Cola Co (NYSE:KO) which is a solid company with a very long history of dividends and growth. I literally had to do nothing to weather this storm.

If I sold my shares of KO, I would *realize* a massive loss. When a stock's value drops suddenly, you lose the value of the stock but still retain the amount shares (ownership) that you hold. You only really see the loss if you sell — *you realize the loss.*

I decided to sell so that I could benefit from claiming that loss on my taxes for the year. I thought it would be great to sell, realize the loss, and immediately buy my shares back.

What I did not know, is there was part of the tax code that prohibits this. If you sell a stock for a loss, the loss is only realized if you do not buy the stock back within a certain number of weeks. As I had sold and bought back within a few days, the IRS does not see that as a realized loss—so no tax benefit.

In hindsight, when I sold KO, I could have bought any number of other solid companies and would have seen the tax advantage that I was looking for.

That said, 2014 was not a good year for me in the market as I ultimately lost just over $10,000 in the market; however, I retained the similar amount in stock value so it was made up in growth in 2015. That year I cleared nearly $9K in the market.

The market gives and it takes. Understanding the ebb and flow of the market is challenging and it is at financial risk to move money around in the markets.

I made the progression from gambling in penny stocks to swing trading in large corporations. In 2016 I changed my interaction with the market in a significant way as I am now truly an investor — not a trader. All of my money is sitting in large corporations that have steady growth and reliable dividends. I am not making money as fast as I was swing trading, but it is safer, has less tax consequences, and, most importantly, I do not have to monitor the market as closely. I can go on enjoying my life and check-in from time to time to count the dividends and make sure the stocks are still growing.

The other way that I invest in the market is through my employer 401(k) retirement plans. If you are fortunate enough to have an employer that offers 401(k) investing, especially if they match contributions, take advantage of it. There are tax benefits to this and it is a great way to grow your net worth for retirement. If your employer matches contributions and you are not putting in the maximum they allow to match, you are throwing away free money.

It's the equivalent of your employer offering you a higher salary and you reject it.

Taking that cut from your take home pay may pinch the monthly budget, but I promise your future self will thank you.

There are risks in the stock market, but there are ways that you can educate yourself to navigate those waters to make money and keep yourself on a lower risk level. I would not rule out the stock market, even if you do not have a lot to invest right away.

There are plenty of online trading companies that allow you to manage your own stock buying and selling at minimal cost. For a few dollars per trade, you can get started putting money away. If you do not have a lot to get started, start small and keep putting money into the market regularly until you have a more substantial number to move around. It doesn't happen overnight, but with careful trading you may see rewarding results.

$$

In March of 2005, I decided to purchase my first home. I had climbed out of the abyss of bankruptcy and my credit was well into the 600s which would be enough to qualify for a mortgage. My girlfriend and I lived in that property until 2009 when she bought a home.

At the time, the US Government was offering a first-time homebuyers tax credit of $8,000. This was a true tax credit that did not need to be repaid. When the government offers $8,000, it is worth looking into the offer.

My girlfriend and I had purchased a home together in 2005, but the entire purchase was done in my name only. That said, she qualified as a first-time homebuyer, so we went shopping.

We found a nicer, larger home in the town right next to ours and the price was right. She made the purchase in here name, grabbed the $8,000, and we were on our way to living in a newer house.

I needed to resolve what to do with "my" property. Having only lived in the house for four years and buying it with no money down, there was not much equity in the property. Worse, the housing bubble had burst and home values had dropped. Not knowing any better, we still listed my house on the market. There was little interest from buyers.

We were now paying mortgages on two properties and looking to heat an empty house through winter. It was not an ideal situation, but I was not interested in losing money on the property.

A few years earlier I had completed my master's degree in student affairs administration and I had been working for a local university. One day, a student told me she was looking at withdrawing from school. She was an older student and explained that she was going through an unpleasant divorce with three kids. She said she had to focus on her family as she wasn't even sure where they were going to live.

As we talked more, I realized how precarious her position was and I brought up my empty home that was a mile from campus. She checked it out and decided to move in.

As this was a help to both of us, the rent was cheap and I needed her to cover the heating costs which she was grateful to do.

That first rent payment was a marvelous experience. It was a true breath of fresh air into a period of some tight finances. She ultimately only stayed in the house for a few months to get back on her feet and helped us through winter.

That experience gave me insight into the world of being a landlord. I saw the potential and pulled the house off the market and we went searching for a new tenant.

Rather quickly we found a marvelous young family that was perfect for our home. The house provided a nice upgrade for them and their growing family. They have been incredible tenants for more than six years and I anticipate they will be staying many more years.

My first foray into rental income has been a success.

$$

I mentioned in the chapter on net worth that throughout 2011 I was reading a lot of books on investing and was looking to purchase a property near my new job that was about an hour away.

Having seen the benefits of rental income, I intentionally sought out a two- or three-unit rental property. My plan was to use one apartment, for myself, a few nights per week when I went to work instead of taking the long commute every day. This would have been especially important during the winter when it snowed.

I found the perfect building and made the purchase. It was two units with a long-term, reliable upstairs tenant and a not-as-reliable tenant on the first floor with a month-to-month lease. This made it easy to move out the bottom floor, renovate, and move into it.

As life turns out, my girlfriend and I made the difficult decision to end our relationship on very amicable terms. She left with her property and the money we had put into it and I left with my old home and my newly purchased building.

Two months before I purchased my building, I had started the net worth calculator. It was terrific to see the immediate change the month following the purchase and to continued growth over the years of maintaining two properties with tenants.

Rent is another avenue to receive financial income. The great thing about rent is that you can apply it directly toward your mortgage payments which relieves a significant bill every month all while building more equity into a major asset—the property. When the mortgage is paid off, then that rental income is very real extra money every month.

I held that property for more than four years until I moved out of the country. That's a story for another chapter. What is relevant here is that I was able to live four-plus years without a monthly, personal housing expense. For my apartment I only needed to cover my utilities and upkeep on the property which allowed me to live a very comfortable life style.

$$

As of now, my income streams are my salary, rental income on the old property, dividends from stock, and some money from book sales each month. I am currently considering buying another rental property.

$$

Yes, I have an Excel sheet that I use to monitor income as well. It is also duplicated on part of the net worth calculator I use. Checking my financial health, at least once per month, is simply part of my routine now.

At any given moment, I know my credit score, my income, and my precise net worth. Just like you might walk around with your head higher and feeling more confident after a positive checkup from your doctor, I live with the confidence of knowing my finances are healthy.

Besides being a tad obsessive about documenting things, I am also very competitive. My primary competition has always been myself — my performance.

I am inspired by improving numbers. This was great when I was racing cars. If it can be measured, it can be improved. I have always been addicted to increasing numbers (or decreasing if that is the goal). Whichever way we would prefer to see a figure go, that is the direction I am headed.

My personal financial goals are to nail a perfect 850 credit score and attain a million dollar net worth. My income goal is to generate enough passive income (rent, stocks, etc.) that work becomes optional. That will happen once passive income is greater than monthly bills.

All three of these goals will be met.

$$

Another reason it is great to know your numbers is to have an understanding of how financially safe you are. If all three of your numbers are good, then you can handle what life throws at you if any of the three falter.

If your income is decent and you have a solid net worth, you can handle a hit to your credit score. If you have good income and a high credit rating, you can build your net worth. If your credit and net worth are great, then losing some income will not be as terrible of an experience.

In one my jobs, we went through five rounds of layoffs in four years. It was a very toxic environment. Stress was everywhere. There were very real concerns about colleagues losing their jobs — and they did.

Many of coworkers, like a lot of Americans, were relying solely on their paychecks to survive. Some of them were also balancing uncomfortable debts on top of that. I felt bad for them and understood why they were so concerned. Losing their job was like losing the foundation in their home. Everything was potentially going to fall in on them that moment.

Like my colleagues, I was worried about losing my job, but I knew I had enough resources and passive income that I could comfortably live with minor adjustments to my lifestyle for the better part of a year. In a worst-case scenario, I could liquidate stocks and live for three to four years if I were more frugal.

In the end, I was not laid off, but the reorganizations did catch up with me. My position was split into two and I was offered to take either of those positions or door #3 which was an attractive buyout. I chose the latter and spent six months traveling while I applied for new positions all over the country and, even a few, outside of the U.S.

$$

Know your numbers. Know your health. Take your financial pulse today. It's okay if you are not pleased with the numbers. It's even okay if you are really upset by the results.

It is just like going to the doctor and being told your lifestyle has been damaging to your health. It is time to make a change. Hopefully the rest of this book will offer some insight into how to live a "healthier" lifestyle.

Chapter 5

Housing: Living Below Your Means
Large Expenses

My friend Joey, the one whose friend had his $20,000 cell phone stolen, has occasionally worked in home finance. He told me a story about traveling to NYC with an attorney that he knew. He was headed to the city to do some paperwork for a client.

Joey said it was a big deal worth millions of dollars. The client owned a pair of pizza shops and had worked out an interesting Real Estate deal. From what Joey understood, the guy worked out a deal to build three units on top of three buildings in lower Manhattan. This was a total of nine units in a terrific neighborhood. They were being built on top of already existing three-unit buildings.

Apparently he had worked out this whole deal on paper and had already pre-sold all nine of the new units. What a fantastic investment for this restaurant owner.

Joey said he got to learn about this guy's path to success. He told Joey that he came to the U.S. from the Middle East when he was 17 years old. At 18 he started driving a taxi.

From what I recall, he was living in some sort of communal housing and was saving his money. He eventually saved enough to buy his own cab. He made the important transition from being an employee to being self-employed.

He stayed in his current living arrangements and kept saving his money. He eventually had enough money that he could buy two more taxis and hire drivers. With two driver's working for him, he was now made the transition from being self-employed to a business owner.

He decided to sell his cab company and look for a different investment. That is when he found a pizza shop for sale in NYC.

He didn't know much about pizza, but he knew something about people. The pizza shop was located in an area with a lot of night clubs — all of which closed at 2:00 a.m.

After buying the pizza shop, he only made one significant change. His shop was now open until 4:00 a.m. to cater to all of the people coming out from a night of clubbing.

He eventually made enough money to invest in a second pizza shop and start looking for other investments. That is when he started working out this plan to build more units on top of these existing buildings.

The night Joey met him they were all siting in a booth in this guy's pizzeria. The line was out the door and this guy had his brand new Mercedes sitting out front. This guy was doing extremely well for himself.

The really incredible part of this rags-to-riches story is that the night Joey met him; this guy was only 23 years old. He accomplished all of that in just more than five years.

Part of this success story, besides patient planning, a dedicated work ethic, and a very smart plan, was this man's willingness to live below his means in order to achieve his financial goals.

I would venture to guess that most young people that were in his position and had started making a good income would have started searching for their own apartment, buying clothes, and look for other "must-have" items. His financial restraint and dedication to savings allowed him to be responsive to opportunity when it presented itself.

Are you willing to live a few years in communal living arrangements in order to save enough cash to invest in your own business?

$$

How many people do you know living beyond their means? Their finances are stretched with high rents (or mortgages), steep car payments, and piles of credit card debt. They are potentially a missed pay check away from financial disaster. Maybe you are too.

How different would life be if everyone chose to live below their means? Living below your means allows you to be more responsive to disruptive situations life throws at you and it allows you to be more flexible when financial opportunities arise.

$$

One of the largest expenditures we have every month is for a roof over our heads. Whether you are renting or paying a mortgage, chances are that is one of your highest bills every month. If you are looking for significant cost savings, wouldn't it make sense to cut one of the largest bills you have?

When I was 15 years old, my mother and my soon-to-be stepfather decided to buy a home together. With their combined incomes, they could have afforded a very nice suburban home, but that was not going to happen.

My mother had learned a lot from her first divorce and she was not going to enter into a situation where she could not afford to keep a house if something happened to her spouse.

She reasoned that it was more logical to buy a decent city home that either of them could afford if something happened to the other. She was compelling them to live below their means so that they would not be strapped if life threw a curve their way.

$$

In 2005, when my girlfriend and I bought that first house, I remembered my mother's argument. I insisted on buying a place that either of us could manage without the other.

At the time, I was renting a 2-bedroom apartment for $600 per month and paying $45 additional rent for two garage spaces. My girlfriend was paying $620 per month for a one-bedroom place.

The mortgage on the house we bought came to $560 per month. Imagine the savings we enjoyed. Yes, we could have bought a significantly nicer house for the $1,265 per month we were spending on rent, but we would not have enjoyed as much disposable income. That huge monthly savings provided me with more money to invest in the stock market.

More importantly, it also provided an opportunity to get ahead on mortgage payments.

$$

It is extremely important to understand mortgages and the terms of any loan you may sign your name on. Too often people go to a bank to determine how much of a mortgage they can afford. That is the equivalent of asking a baker how much cake you can eat. It is in their interest, *not yours,* to sell you more. Loans are a way banks make money.

Yes, they have an interest in ensuring that you can actually make the payments on your mortgage, but it is not their concern if you can still afford nice vacations, gift giving at holidays, or dinner out whenever you wish.

$$

My friends Ron and Jess are a married couple and were living in an apartment complex. They were dealing with all of the challenges of apartment living (small spaces, shared parking, neighbors against every wall, etc.).

They were ready to buy their first home. I remember Jess's excitement when she told me they were pre-approved for $135,000 mortgage. I congratulated her on her good fortunate and inquired if they started looking at homes.

She said they had and the Realtor was showing them some really exciting properties in the $145,000–$165,000 range. My heart sank. I could see the financial trap that is set for many Americans: talk to the banker to find out how much you can spend and then talk to a Realtor that will nudge you beyond that number. It is a recipe for economic hardship and, with one unlucky life event, potentially financial disaster.

I asked Jess if she and Ron would be willing to sit down with me one night to discuss their plan for purchasing a home. I said I was willing to spring for dinner and I just wanted them to hear me out before they made any home purchase. She agreed and we enjoyed a wonderful evening going over some excel sheets I prepared in regards to mortgages.

When I asked Jess and Ron what they were looking for, they said they wanted to find their first home together that would last them for many years. They didn't want to be moving any more. They were excited about doing home projects and fixing up a place the way they wanted. After years of apartment living, they were ready to make a place their own.

They had already looked online at properties in the $125,000–$140,000 range and, not surprisingly, the Realtor took them out to see $145,000–$165,000 homes. They were excited about what they were seeing.

I asked if they looked at any $80,000–$100,000 homes. The look I received was almost comical. Why would someone look that far below their range? That price point would probably keep them in the city more than they would like. How awful would houses be that cost so little?

I asked them to keep an open mind.

I showed Jess and Ron two options.

House 1: This is what the bank said they could afford. The bank indicated they could afford a $135,000 mortgage. They had 3%, $4,000 for down money, which meant they would be borrowing $131,000.

I am not sure what interest rate they were actually quoted. I am using 4.5% for illustrative purposes only.

With a typical 30-year-mortgage at 4.5% interest they would be looking at an initial monthly principal, interest, taxes, and insurance (PITI) payments of $963.55. After 106 months, they could have the house assessed to get rid of the private mortgage insurance (PMI). Remember, PMI, is required until you have 20% equity in the home. After getting rid of PMI, their monthly payment would drop down to $854.38.

House 2: This is the option I proposed they consider. Look for a home around $90,000. With their $4,000 down payment, they would now be putting down 4.4% instead of 3%. This would get them out of PMI quicker.

With a typical 30-year-mortgage at 4.5% interest they would be looking at initial monthly PITI payments of $651.17. After 101 months, they could have the house assessed to get rid of PMI which would drop payments down to $579.50.

Comparison: House 1 was a nicer, more valuable property, but came with monthly payments that were $312.38 higher than House 2. Over the course of the loans, House 1 would cost $96,162.79 in interest compared to $63,631.44 for House 2. That is $32,531.35 more in interest! Do you see why it is in the bank's interest for you to borrow more?

Let's not forget the PMI. House 1 will require $11,790.00 in PMI payments compared to House 2's payments of $7,238.33 — that is $4,551.67 in savings.

I asked Jess and Ron, "What could you do with an extra $300 per month?" Their eyes lit up and they shared a terrific smile.

It could be a car payment (I hope not, as I am not a fan of borrowing for auto purchases). $300 is a nice amount to set aside for vacations and travel.

They mentioned a desire to do house projects. Where was that money coming from if they maxed out a housing payment?

That extra money could also be used to get ahead on their mortgage and pay their house off sooner and save a lot in interest payments. Remember, they were told they could afford $950 per month payments. What if they still made that payment on the less expensive home? What affect would that have on their borrowing?

$$

What most people do not realize is that if you can make an extra mortgage payment every year and spread it over 12 months, you can drop nearly 5 years off your mortgage.

If Jess and Ron bought House 2 whose monthly mortgage was $651.17, spreading out an "extra" payment over the course of a year would be an extra $54.25 per month.

What would they get for that? They would pay their house off 5 years sooner, pay more than $5,000 less in interest, and get rid of the PMI more than 2 years sooner. If life changed and that extra $54 per month became a burden, they could simply revert to the basic mortgage payment.

Could they do that with House 1? With House 1, they *have to make* those higher payments. They most likely would not have much wiggle room in their monthly budget to pay extra as they borrowed the max of what the bank said they could afford.

What if Ron and Jess purchased House 2, but made the $963.55 monthly payments the bank said they could afford on House 1?

They would eliminate the PMI in just two years (instead of 8.5) and they would pay their house off in just more than nine years! Along the way, they also would save nearly $35,000 in interest payments.

$$

In the end, Jess and Ron bought the $90,000 property. They were pleasantly surprised at the options in that price range in the city. The last time I visited them, they had just finished remodeling one room and were excited to tell me their plans for other spaces around the house. It was clear they enjoyed home projects and they most likely would not have had the funds to do that in the more expensive place.

My advice to them was to settle on a mortgage that was well below their means. It offered less monthly stress making payments and provided a fantastic opportunity to get ahead on payments.

$$

In 2011 when I was looking at buying two- or three-unit buildings, I was very aware that I would be going back to "apartment living." This time was going to be different though. This time I would be the landlord. This time, I would l have control over my own place. This time, I would be collecting the rent—not paying it.

The building I purchased was originally 3 stories high with a basement. It was connected to another building next door of similar design. Both properties had been renovated into multiple apartments from an original one-home layout.

In my building, my tenant had the top two floors and I had a one-bedroom first-floor unit with basement access. This was a considerable down-size of space from the large home from which I had just moved.

I could occasionally hear my tenant upstairs moving around or her cat scampering across the floor. At times, I could hear the neighbors through the wall.

This new property only had on-street parking, unlike the garage I had at my old home. Thankfully our street was not overly full so finding parking was rarely an issue. It was something that you had to deal with when the snow came.

Overall, these discomforts were not too terrible. I could have easily afforded a really nice home in the 'burbs so what kept me living happily in my small apartment? I often thought about the guy in NYC that my friend Joey met. I tried imaging the communal living arrangements he accepted as shelter for the few years he was saving to start a business. I often found solace in the fact that I was probably living more comfortably than he was.

If he could do it, so could I. I took pleasure in having a tenant cover most of my living expenses and watching my net worth calculator grow each month. My liability column, which included mortgages on two properties, shrank at a faster rate with three incomes (mine and two tenants) paying down the mortgages.

This also allowed me to pay extra on my mortgages and get ahead on those payments which, consequently, increased my credit score.

I owned that building for 4.5 years. By monitoring my monthly financial health numbers, it was clear that buying that second rental property allowed me to increase income ($7,200 per year), grow my net worth (more than $100,000 in four years), and raise my credit rating (nearly 100 points). I saved enough on housing expenses that I was able to afford to visit all 50 states. All of that occurred in fewer than five years. This was all possible because I chose to live below my means.

Maybe that is what is meant by a "healthy investment?"

Let's say you buy that car today for $16,906 and the next day you decide to sell it. If you look at Kelley Blue Book, their suggested value on the car is now $14,759.

You lost $2,147 in value the moment you took the keys and drove off the lot! That would be bad enough if you paid cash, but how many people borrow for a new car purchase?

Assuming you have no money down and no trade in, you will need a car loan for the full price. My bank is currently listing new car loans for 3.09% APR for three years *if you qualify* (I hope you have that good credit rating!).

This will give you a $492 monthly payment. In three years, when the car is paid off, you will have paid $793 in interest so that actual price you paid for the car was $17,699.

I assure you, the Kelley Blue Book price will be significantly less in three years. So many people finance a new car purchase and they are giving up a lot of their net worth for the luxury of being the first person to own a car.

This calamity of finances only gets worse at the dealership. You are excited about buying a new car, emotions are high, and the salesperson tells you that you are approved and that your payments will be $492 per month. Dread sets in as you realize you can't afford a payment that high — *probably because you bought a home that the bank swore you could afford and you are suffocating under mortgage payments.*

You politely thank the salesman and inform them that you can't afford the car after all. With a smile in their face, and a sparkle in their eye, the salesman quickly comes to the rescue with this line, "How much of a payment can you afford?"

Meekly you indicate that you were hoping for a $250 monthly payment which is nearly half of the proposed loan payment. The salesman says wait right here and runs off to the finance department.

A few minutes later they return with exciting news. You are approved for a monthly payment of $257! The salesperson is your hero — your friend! You can now afford this brand new car!!

This is all very exciting. They make sure the tank is full and stuff a couple of certificates in your hand for free oil changes. You are out the door in your new ride and eager to take some photos of this baby for your Facebook page.

What just happened there? How was that possible? How did the payments go from $492/month to $257/month?! Did the price suddenly get cut in half?

No. Not all. The dealership just approved you for a 72-month (six-year) loan instead of a 36-month (three-year) loan.

Did this magic wand change anything with the *value* of your purchase? You better believe it did.

With the stated interest rate, over the course of 6 years, you are now paying $1,588 in interest. That brings the actual price of the car to $18,494. Don't forget that when you drove off the lot, the car immediately lost value and was actually worth $14,759.

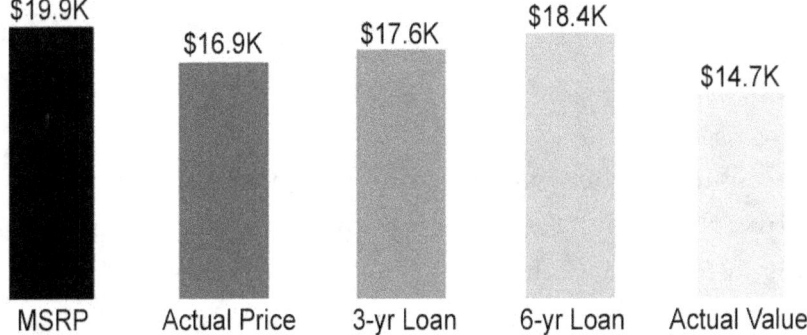

This gets even worse when you factor in that the car will not be paid off for six years. By that time, it will most likely have at least 80,000 miles on it — *if it was not wrecked, stolen, or vandalized.* It will have lost a ton of value the entire time you were making payments.

$$

Cars are a necessary evil. Newer-model, gently-used cars are a somewhat better choice — probably the best choice. If the car is new enough and nice enough, the price still may require the need for a loan and you are right back to the math of financing something that loses value.

More often than not, I buy slightly older cars and accept that I would have car problems from time to time. To balance that out, I would own 2 or 3 at a time. Buying older models allowed me to pay cash and not deal with loans. It also provided cheaper insurance. In fact, depending on the car, I might eliminate collision/comprehensive insurance all together and just purchase the required liability policy.

This is the best answer that I have come up with for buying cars — which are always bound to be losing purchases.

$$

It might not be evident from reading this, but I am a retired "car guy." Growing up and for most of my life, I was infatuated with cars. The love of cars, led me to purchasing many sports cars over the years.

I went through a phase where I always kept a damp towel and dry towel in my car so I could wipe the slightest dirt off of the car when I parked. Parked? Yes, when I parked, it had to be far from other cars in the place of most safety.

There were times in college that I would leave parties to go check on my car. My friends teased me, "Is it still there?"

Through my twenties, a large portion of my income went into buying, altering, repairing and replacing cars. This all led to an exciting period of my life with Jekyl Hyde Racing when I was having a ton of fun modifying and racing cars.

During those years I had several cars wrecked. I had one car stolen and lit on fire. One of my cars was vandalized with key scratches. When I went to the shop after it was fixed, I found that it had been keyed again in their lot. I had four different sports cars get backed into while they were parked.

My love affair with cars abruptly changed, like a light switch being flipped, at the end of my last racing season. I suddenly realized that for the better part of two decades, my cars *owned me*.

When I cashed out on the racing business, I was able to start making all of that money work for me. I had a real sense of the cost associated with playing with cars for so many years.

In the year's right after racing, I still wanted a nice car. I bought used BMWs that were just a few years old. They were stylish, had performance, and I did not have to stress about them. They were just cars.

A few years ago I moved to a tiny island in the Caribbean and purchased an "island car." Island cars suit me just fine. They are old, beat up, and get us from point A to point B.

It requires no washing, no worries on parking, and doing the minimum to keep is running is just fine. Car-related spending was once my largest monthly expense. Now it is almost nothing.

In fact, our island car is actually my wife's. When I first arrived on island I bought a brand new scooter for $2,500 U.S. and it costs about $3 per week in gas.

If I were back in the states, I would try to live somewhere that I could walk or use a bicycle to get to work. I might consider living somewhere with good public transportation.

Realistically, I would probably still have a car, but I am certain it would not be a very nice one. Cars are simply not things I value any more.

Chapter 7

Taxes: An Optional Expense
Large Expenses

If you ask most people what is their largest monthly expense, they will most likely say their housing bill, whether it is rent or mortgage payments. In actuality, for many people, their largest monthly expense is probably taxes.

In the U.S., Federal income is going to be taxed at a rate of 15-28% for most people reading this book. Most states also have an income tax. Depending on which state you live in, that rate will most likely be an additional 3-9%. On top of those two big numbers, you might also have a local, municipality, or city income tax that could run another percent or two.

All combined, you may very well be seeing upwards of 40% of your income being taken away in taxes. That is why I say for many people, it is your largest monthly expense.

People do not see it that way since the money is usually taken from them before they ever see it. We tend to only think about the money we have left *after taxes have been taken* out of our pay check, but the reality is that was your money too.

$$

I run my life like a business. If there is a way to cut expenses and improve profit, I am going to look into it and so should you.

To see the biggest gains, it makes sense to tackle the largest expenses. We already discussed property and automobiles. It is time to look at taxes.

It is worth noting that I am not a tax account, not am I tax law attorney. I'm a slight above average guy who has done a lot of homework. That said; double-check my work with an appropriate accountant or attorney before you follow any advice given here.

Benjamin Franklin once said, "In this world nothing can be said to be certain, except death and taxes." We tend to live under that assumption, but the truth is, Mr. Franklin was only half right — only death is certain. Taxes are avoidable, at least to some degree.

$$

I did not pay any Federal income taxes for the tax year 2006 and I sleep quite comfortably. I have no fear the IRS is going to come looking for me. I've done nothing wrong.

Even though I earned nearly $38,000 that year, the IRS required no taxes from me. Since I already had taxes withheld all year, I actually received a 100% tax return from Uncle Sam. That's right. They gave me all of *my money* back.

I recall going into my accountant in early 2007 with a huge smile on my face. She commented on my good spirit for coming to my annual tax meeting. I proudly informed her that she would be getting all of my taxes back for me this year.

She laughed and said that was doubtful. She informed me that the only people who managed to get a full refund had low incomes and lots of children.

I conceded that I wasn't certain that she would be getting back all of my taxes, but I was confident that it would be a good tax return that year.

Why was I so sure? I was confident because I had been learning about all sorts of tax deductions. It is really worth your time to learn about all possible deductions that you can claim and take full advantage of them to maximize your return. It is your right to do so.

Having bought my first home in the previous year, 2006 was the first full year that I could claim deductions on my mortgage. I also had been paying on my student loans and that interest was also deductible. That year was also the last full year of my grad program. Tuition on advanced degrees is tax deductible. So, 2006 was also one of the more significant years for me to claim a loss on my Jekyl Hyde Racing business.

When my accountant finished entering all of my numbers into her system, she sat back and simply said, "huh." That was followed by, "I don't believe it. You *are* getting back all of your taxes."

Educate yourself on deductions and see how well you can position yourself. You may never see a full refund, but every dollar counts.

$$

There are currently seven states that have no personal income taxes: Alaska, Florida, Nevada, South Dakota, Texas, Washington and Wyoming. Interestingly, Alaska pays its residents from its oil wealth trust fund every year. Some years it has been more than $2,000 just for living the entire year in the state.

My understanding is that New Hampshire and Tennessee only tax dividends and investment income, not your regular pay.

Before you rush to move to one of these nine states, educate yourself on the entire financial picture of these locations. The states obviously need revenue to operate and if it is not coming from income taxes, you can be certain they are taxing something else (sales, gas, etc.).

$$

My now favorite tax deduction, which truly takes the cake (and the ice cream to go with it) is the Foreign Earned Income Exclusion (FEIE).

From www.irs.gov:

> "If you are a U.S. citizen or a resident alien of the United States and you live abroad, you are taxed on your worldwide income. However, you may qualify to exclude from income up to an amount of your foreign earnings that is adjusted annually for inflation ($92,900 for 2011, $95,100 for 2012, $97,600 for 2013, $99,200 for 2014 and $100,800 for 2015). In addition, you can exclude or deduct certain foreign housing amounts."

Basically what that section says is that if you live outside of the United States and make less than $100,000 you do not owe U.S. Federal taxes. This offsets the taxes you would be paying in the country you are living and working in.

This wonderful deduction was not the reason I accepted a position in another country, but I was very pleased to learn about it. My interest was piqued even more when I learned that the country I was moving to is one of about two dozen that has no income tax at all. That said I am not currently paying any personal Federal income taxes. Since I am not residing in a U.S. state, there is also no state or local income taxes to worry about.

Touché Ben Franklin.

Yes, it is true that the sales tax where I am is high, as are the taxes on flights and automobile purchases, but those taxes I accept when I choose to spend my money — not by going to work.

If you are willing to live in another country, and are not making 6 figures, you just might be able to remove the tax man's shackles. Even if you are making in the 6s, you could drop a huge chunk of taxes.

Chapter 8

Shopping: Managing to Save Money
Large Expenses

Who doesn't love shopping? Buying that shiny new "must-have" item is such an adrenaline rush. We feel the excitement to get this new thing home and open it up.

Maybe we can't wait to tell our friends and families about this new purchase. Maybe we are excited to wear it, display it, collect it, or simply use it.

I'll fair warn you that, just like I lost my love for autos, my desire for shopping also has vanished. That isn't actually fair to say. I still really enjoy shopping. What I've lost is my desire for *stuff*. Shopping is still part of my life, but buying, not so much.

I used to be an avid shopper. You might even say I was addicted to shopping. Along the way I learned a few things about saving money and getting the most out my shopping experience. I will share my tips with you here, but will not be using them as much myself.

Like cars, "stuff" will most likely end up damaged, lost, stolen, or become obsolete. Another problem with "things," as my mother likes to point out before a purchase, is it will need to be cleaned or dusted. My mother often asks, "How many times do you want to pick that *thing* up the rest of your life to dust it?"

These considerations started me questioning purchases, but the real big changed happened for me when I decided to move out of the U.S. There was a need to cull the insane volume of "stuff" I had bought over the years before making an international move.

I thought it would be sad to sell so many of my coveted "things." The idea of renting a storage shed crossed my mind, but I quickly recalled that I avoid anything with a monthly payment. That was not going to happen.

As I decided the "must stays" and the "must goes," I realized how cathartic this experience was. I had moved a lot in my life and all of this "stuff" was cleaned, boxed, labeled, moved, unpacked, put away, and not really used more times than I care to count.

The idea of doing a big move and not having to unpack all of my "things" was becoming very attractive. In the end, I still brought way too much with me and I know in my heart that I will be selling even more the next time I move. I am just not as fond of "stuff" as I used to be.

If you have never heard the comedian George Carlin's skit on "stuff," it is worth a listen.

Assuming that I have not squelched your desire for "stuff," and you are interested in saving money on your purchases, read on for my suggestions to keep more of your money in your pocket.

$$

Before we can even start talking about saving money shopping, we need to discuss the best way to pay for purchases. If you are paying cash, then you are missing out on discounts on nearly every purchase you make. Credit cards have become incredibly competitive and there are all sorts of cards that have cash-back or points incentives for use. It is worth taking the time to read the fine print.

I strongly advise finding the card that works best for you and use that one on as many of your purchases as you can to maximize the rewards. Once you find the card that is right for you, make sure you read all of the options for redemption as you might be able increase your returns on your cash back.

In 2008 I opened a charge card with Discover as I had a friend who was constantly talking about what he was going to buy with his "cash back" money from Discover. Always having been intrigued by free money, I investigated and applied for one of their cards that did not have an annual fee and offered 1% cash back on purchases.

Until I moved out of the country, I used my Discover card for everything — *everything*. If the option was available to pay with a credit card, I used the Discover. The only time I did not use the card is if I was somewhere that only took cash or did not accept Discover. Unfortunately there are places that do not accept Discover which, sadly, includes almost everywhere in the country I am currently residing.

There are a few reasons that I bought everything I could on my Discover card. First, it makes life simpler that you basically pay everything once per month with your credit card statement. Secondly, you are getting back 1% on everything you buy and it adds up. It is like a monthly savings account so even the quick stop for snacks at a gas station add up to something.

If you do this, it is imperative that you pay off the entire balance every month. If you carry a balance, the interest will consume any positive movement you made financially and you are just giving the creditor free money. Do not carry balances on your card. I have been with Discover since 2009 and I have not paid a single penny in interest.

Discover also offers free updated credit scores every month which helps me monitor my credit health. You can also set alerts for certain types of transactions which can notify you of potential fraud on your account.

I just logged into my account and looked at my spending on Discover for the last 48 months (four years). For the last 20 months, I have been living outside of the U.S. so I have not been able to use my Discover as much. Most of my purchases on the card now are for booking airlines and accommodations (more on that in the chapter on travel). Even with the current prohibitions on using the card, I have charged $110,155.00 on my Discover card in the last 48 months.

With 1% cash back, that comes to $1,101.55 or roughly $275 per year. What could you do with an extra $275? You could invest it, you could pay down the principal on your mortgage, apply it to a vacation. There are lots of things you could do with that money.

I chose to not accept the cash back. As mentioned previously, read the fine print on redemption. Instead of taking cash back, Discover has partner gift cards available for trade in and the partners will give you *more than the face value* of your cash back.

For years, my preferred partner gift cards came from Staples. Up until a few months ago, if you gave Staples $20 of your cash back from Discover, they would give you a $25 gift card — a 25% raise! That drastically increased my $1,100 cash back to $1,375 (nearly $350 per year).

Staples recently changed the offer to $30 for $25 changed in. Although it seems like you are still getting a free $5 you are paying a bit more for it. I am now getting a 20% raise instead of $25. It is still a terrific deal.

Discover has over 130 partners — all offering different incentives to cash in with them. I wonder what deals you could find to combine.

$$

I mentioned that my current country is not very Discover friendly which has lead me to paying cash for more purchases than I would like. My wife and I also are doing a lot of international traveling and Discover is just not as widely accepted as Visa.

I have had a Visa card through Capital One longer than Discover. In fact, I have kept that account open specifically for the history of the account—credit history length positively affects your credit score. It was also a useful card to have when Discover was not accepted but it does not have any cash-back incentives.

My move out of the country has made using the Capital One card problematic for purchasing some items — specifically airfare. When I make a transaction outside of the U.S., for some international airlines, Capital One's fraud detection kicks in and declines the payment. This results in me having to call Capital One and go through the transaction all over again, while sitting on an international call.

I have had to do this too many times and between Capital One not giving cash back and actually costing me money in calls to make basic transactions, it has become problematic for my current living situation. That said, it was time to find a new Visa card.

After doing some research and talking to other travelers, I applied for the Bank of America Travel Rewards credit card. Unlike other credit cards that offer airline miles, this card allows you to build travel points that can be used for any airline. They even allow the credits to be used on hotels, tolls, rental cars, and entrance fees to some tourist sites.

Instead of cash back, it offers 1.5 points for every $1 spent. Those points get cashed in at 1% For every 2,500 points, you get $250 toward travel purchases.

This is a better deal for me since with Discover I was getting 1% and increasing that to 1.2% with Staples, but I had to make my purchases at Staples. Now I am earning 1.5% and can use it at a lot of different places. Visa is also more widely accepted.

Bank of America gave me 20,000 points for signing up which equated to $200 toward my travels. The Bank of

America Travel Rewards credit card also offers free admission to hundreds of museums during the first weekend of every month.

All of those math classes and reading the fine print really does pay off. Search out a credit card that makes sense for you and offers rewards that will benefit you. Once you find that card, charge as many of your expenses on it as you can and be sure to pay it off in full each month.

$$

Now that we have the credit card question answered, let's go shopping.

It's expensive to be alive, but I'll take it over the alternative. Just because something costs a lot, doesn't mean you have to pay that price.

There is no shame in coupon shopping or scouring the internet for discount codes for online purchases. It also makes sense to learn and fully understand loyalty programs with different retailers.

If you are not grabbing coupons or using loyalty programs, you are probably spending more than you have to. I used to think coupons were not worth my time. Why hunt around for a coupon to save 50 cents? My time was worth more than that and, it is true, I will not be on "Extreme Couponing" anytime soon. However, I do find that it is worth my time to search for coupons and the best deals when I am making large purchases (more than $100). I tend to go after the big wins.

I have found that it is best to look at combining as many deals as you possibly can to get the best price.

$$

Let's look at an example. We'll use Staples.

I already mentioned how I would transfer my Discover cash back into Staples gift cards. That basically feels like free money since I was getting that in rewards for everything else I already was buying anyway.

The store has its own incentive program called Staples Rewards. When you sign up for this program there is no fee and they give you 2-5% back on your in-store purchases depending on how much you spend per year. I often spent enough ($1,000/year) to make it to their premier level which offered the maximum of 5% back.

Staples also has some amazing sales and monthly coupons. You can find the coupons on their Website or in the circular at the front of the store.

I have a laptop that I bought at Staples. The original price was $275. It was on sale for $225 and Staples published a $75 off laptop coupon which included clearance items. This brought the price down to $150. I presented the cashier with six gift cards that I received from Discover and my Staples Rewards card.

I bought that laptop for the price of the sales tax, which I paid for on my Discover (so the cycle would start to repeat itself toward more gift cards).

In my home state of Pennsylvania, the sales tax is 6% so the tax on the laptop was $13.50. Remember, I also presented my Staples Reward card for the purchase so Staples sent me a rewards certificate for 5% ($11.25) of my purchase. They actually gave me money back for using the money they gave me. I also received 1% back from Discover on the sales tax which would have been 14¢.

My out-of-pocket expense was $2.11. It felt like I paid less than 1% of the price of the laptop.

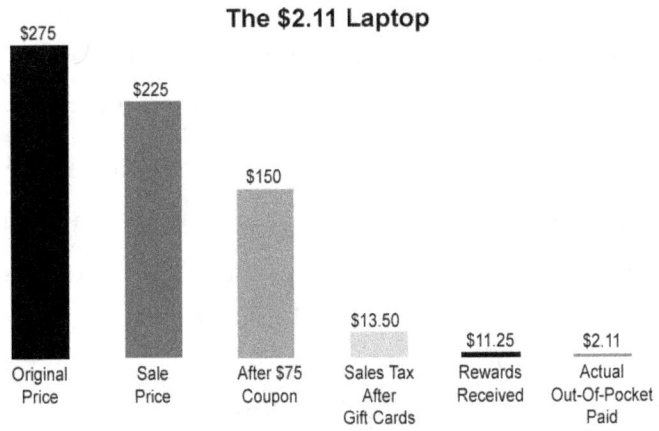

I repeated this cycle for years with Discover/Staples, and bought countless cameras, printers, USB drives, external hard drives, computers, monitors, etc. If it was electronics, I always look to purchase through Staples. I was taking advantage of this deal so often, and to such a great extent, that I felt obliged to go to different Staples locations to make my purchases.

Staples does not typically have the *best price*, but they often have the *best deals* for the savvy shopper that is willing to combine discounts and incentives.

I offer my experience with Staples and Discover Card as an illustration of the possibilities of combing incentives and discounts. Discover has more than a hundred other partners that offer money back on gift cards and each of them may offer their own specialty sales/coupons/incentives. Who knows what you can combine until you look?

$$

There is something to be said for being creative with combing incentives, discounts, sales, and coupons. I find it fascinating how much can be taken off the "original" price. My biggest score by percentage of original price, not in actual dollars saved, was a fitted Van Heusen men's dress shirt.

The original price on the tag was $45. I bought this particular shirt off of a clearance rack, on a sale weekend, with an employee discount and a coupon for a percentage off my entire purchase. When I looked at the final, itemized receipt, I got that shirt for 37¢.

$$

That brings me to another aspect of shopping — bragging. Many people get satisfaction from sharing the details of a new purchase, specifically its price. What aspect of the price is worth sharing?

In 2005 when I bought my first home, I went out to buy a new television. This was an interesting purchase for me as I got rid of cable (and any other sort of paid TV programming) back in 1992*.

> *Over the last 25 years of not paying for TV programming I estimate that I have saved over $25,000. How is that for curbing monthly expenses? ... but I digress.

Let's get back to 2005 and my TV purchase. Large LCD flat-screen TVs had been the hot item for a while and I was very glad to get rid of a cumbersome console TV. Although I did not have TV channels, I did have an extensive movie collection which provides a lot of enjoyment (no, I did not buy brand new movies, I bought used DVDs for $1-$3!).

I was looking at a 42" TV that was retailing for around $2,000. That is a big chunk of change and there is no way that I would spend that kind of money on a TV. I was patient and watched the pricing at several stores.

I ultimately bought the television from Best Buy. It had recently been marked down and I was almost ready to make the purchase when I saw that Best Buy was going to have a big sale weekend and I found a coupon online for a discount on TVs. I walked out of the store with the television for under $850.

I was thrilled with this purchase and later that evening I called a friend to boast about my deal. Ironically, they spoke first and excitedly shared that they just bought a brand new 42" LCD flat screen TV! They were ecstatic that they got the newest version of the SONY TV that just became available. They were proud that they spent $2,200 on this television!

Twelve years later, I am still happily enjoying my TV and the price I paid for it. When the lights are out, the surround sound is on, and the brilliant color lights up, I can't even tell that it does not say SONY on it.

So, where do you see yourself? Are you quick to boast about the deal you snagged or brag about paying top dollar for the latest? I prefer to emphasize what I *saved*, not what I *spent*.

$$

Let's look at another perspective on paying the price for the latest and greatest item.

In 2002 I bought the videogame *Grand Theft Auto III* (please don't judge) for my PlayStation 2. I really enjoyed the game and had a blast playing it.

Meanwhile, my co-worker Kevin had just purchased the next sequel of the series, *Grand Theft Auto: Vice City*. The game was just released and he bought it new for $45.

Every day at worked we shared stories about what was going on in our respective games. He reminisced about all the scenes I was now experiencing for the first time. He got to share how much cooler the new game was with improved graphics, better soundtrack, and larger map (playing area).

I remember those conversations vividly and we were both equally excited about our game play, but one of us paid significantly more (500% more to be exact!) for the same smiles. Imagine that scenario multiplied out across all of the games Kevin and I purchased. He always wanted the new one and I was buying last year's used "must-have" games.

Roughly 2 years later came the release of *Grand Theft Auto: San Andreas*. This was available on the PlayStation 2 or the newer, fancier PlayStation 3. As you may have guessed,

Kevin had already purchased a PS3 and was eagerly awaiting the release of *San Andreas*.

In fact, Kevin was so excited about the release of this game, that he boasted that he stopped by EB Games and paid $10 to reserve a copy of the game on the release date. Imagine that! He was willing to spend $10 for the luxury of buying this game on the first possible day it was available for $50!

He spent $60 on that game and that same week I bought *Vice City*, used, for $10. I was having Kevin's last year's fun for a fraction of the price.

I tried explaining the logic to Kevin and show him how much money he could be saving. I reasoned that he spent more on that one game than I spent on the five games that I owned. His only reply was, "I can't wait to play. I can't wait knowing that it is out there and I am not playing it."

This all comes down to the concept of delayed gratification. Stanford University did a very interesting and insightful study in the '60s/'70s on this topic with children. You can research the "Stanford Marshmallow Experiment" for more details and the findings.

The short answer is that if you are willing to wait, last year's model (or the year before last year) will usually be cheaper than the latest, greatest newfangled thing — especially if you are willing to buy used.

Chapter 9

Traveling: It Doesn't Have to be Expensive
Large Expenses

I am addicted to traveling and it is apparently contagious because my wife seems to have caught it from me. There can be a big price tag on travel or maybe there isn't. It really depends on when, where, and how you travel.

Between June of 2013 and June of 2014 I ran a 5K in all 50 States. It was a personal mission dedicated to a friend of mine. Once I decided to go for that goal, I had to start planning on how I was going to logistically make it happen and strategize how I was going to pay for it.

Whenever you analyze a financial puzzle to find cost savings, go after the big ticket items first. That is where you most likely can score your biggest savings as there is more room to negotiate a deal.

With travel, flights tend to be the most expensive item. If you are traveling for an extended period of time, then accommodations might head to the top of the expense list.

The next most costly aspects of travel are rental cars and/or fuel followed by food. Somewhere in that mix is also entertainment (tickets, entry fees, etc.).

Let's explore some of these to see what kind of cost savings can be found.

$$

The first time I flew on a plane I was 29-years-old and I only got on that plane because my employer paid for the flight. I did not have a fear of flying. It just never occurred to me that I could get on planes and fly places.

Growing up from extremely humble means, it always felt like airlines were for wealthy people or those that saved a long time for a very special trip.

I grew up and lived most of my life in Pennsylvania. My world of travel centered on driving. I've always explored and when I got my first car the United States interstate system was my gateway to everywhere.

Before I turned 21, I explored more than 15 states by car. Most of the states east of the Mississippi were traveled through and I never had a need to leave the ground.

Even after that first flight at 29, I did not fly much. In fact, I only had one personal trip and maybe half of a dozen business trips by the time I was 39.

Half way through being 39, I declared my intent to run a 5K in all 50 states in a year. Clearly I was going to need to be buying more plane tickets, which meant I was going to have to find cheaper ways to do it.

$$

When I traveled the 50 states, I aimed to move quickly and as inexpensively as I could. That said, I had no airline loyalty. I would not be surprised if I had at least one trip on most airlines operating inside the U.S.

Being new to flying, I signed up for every airline's frequent-flyer program not realizing that it is really only beneficial if you are a frequent flyer on one airline. I racked up a ton of useless miles because they were spread out.

Today I concentrate most of my domestic flying with American Airlines (AA). I had racked up points on US Airways and AA while running the 50 states. Afterward, AA and US Airways merged as did my miles.

The tiny island I now live in the Caribbean also has daily AA flights so it has been beneficial for my situation to concentrate my flying with AA.

If you want to travel regularly, pick an airline that has a good rewards program. I would specifically make sure they have miles that do not expire.

I am also open about using the seriously low-cost airlines like Spirit. They offer no extras, not even water and that is fine by me. I can deal with an uncomfortable seat and no beverage to save several hundred dollars.

$$

Where to go to book flights? There are plenty of booking sights online to choose from and I have not investigated which one has the best deal. I loyally have been using Orbitz unless an airline, such as Spirit, is offering a sale right through their Website.

I use Orbitz because of their Orbitz Rewards program. One of the main features of the program is their Orbucks.

Orbucks are earned at the rate of 1% of the cost of flights and vacations or up to 5% of eligible hotels.

The Orbucks can be used directly as cash value on their Website when booking hotels. Ove the last few years, I have earned $631.69. That is a lot of money towards hotel rooms just for booking trips I was planning anyway.

You might be thinking that I am paying more for flights on Orbitz in order to get that money back, but I have often price-matched between Orbitz and the airline directly and the prices have been the same or better on Orbitz.

If you have been following my finances, it should be no surprise that I used to always pay for my flights on Orbitz with my Discover card so I could buy electronics at Staples. My card of choice on the site is now my Bank of America travel card so I can keep booking travel. Between Bank of America and Orbitz, I will be receiving what feels like free hotel rooms from time to time.

$$

When picking flights, if you are firm on the airport you are flying from, the dates you are leaving, and the airport you are flying into, you will have very little room to search for best prices. If you are flexible on dates and willing to drive an hour or two to a different airport, you might be able to score some real bargains. I don't mind driving and I am more than happy to drive up to 2 hours on either end of a trip to save a few hundred dollars.

Living in central Pennsylvania, my closest airport was Harrisburg International (HIA). It was an extremely convenient 15-minute drive and it was a relatively small airport so parking and security were never a challenge. It was even easy to get friends or family to pick me up or drop me off.

Regardless of that convenience, whenever I priced flights, I always looked for bargains from Philadelphia International Airport (PHL) and Baltimore–Washington International Airport (BWI).

This tactic was especially important for international flights as I have found better deals from Washington Dulles International Airport (IAD) and even the New York City airports John F. Kennedy International Airport (JFK), LaGuardia Airport (LGA), and Newark Liberty International Airport (EWR).

The same is true on the other end of your trip. I have flown into Las Vegas, NV to start a road trip through Utah; Portland, OR to explore Seattle, WA, Dallas, TX to visit Arkansas and Oklahoma; and I have landed in Minneapolis, MN to sightsee in Wisconsin and Iowa.

The same is true for international travel. We recently took a trip to Italy. Having never been there before, it did not matter to us which airport we came into. We were able to price tickets over a variety of Italian cities to find the best pricing to start our exploring. In fact, we even price some nearby countries to see if we could save money and explore something else while we were there.

This logic, and savings, gets expanded if you are planning a trip with multiple destinations. This type of trip allows you the opportunity to alter the order of airports visited and the dates. By negotiating an day or two more or less in each location, you can drastically affect the price of your ticket.

The more flexible you can be the better rates you may find. I do not see these alternative routes that put us out of our way as inconveniences, but rather serendipitous opportunities to explore the unexpected.

$$

Another way you can save money with flying is to break a larger trip up into smaller segments as you might get better pricing on smaller components.

Here is an example: I just looked on Orbitz for booking a two-week trip from Miami through three capital cities of South America: Santiago, Chile, Buenos Aires, Argentina, and Montevideo, Uruguay. This is actually a trip my wife and I did last year.

If I select the preferred travel dates and book this as one giant trip, the price comes out to $1,806.56.

If, however, I book the Miami segments as one trip (Miami to Santiago and then returning to Miami from Montevideo) the price for that segment is $1,367.66. I still need to get to Uruguay from Chile via Buenos Aries, Argentina. Those two flights, that come up as direct flights from a local carrier are only $265.58.

The combined price of those two segments is $1,633.24! Booking two separate trips instead of one just saved $173.32 for the exact same flights and dates.

What if you did not care about the order of the countries visited? Entering into Orbitz the same trip dates, but switching the order to start with Uruguay and ending with Chile and still booking as one giant trip, the price is now only $1,518.56 saving another $114.68.

Now what happens if we break that giant trip up into two segments? The Miami to Montevideo trip, with a return to Miami form Chile is $1,213.56. The smaller segment jumping across the countries with a few days in Argentina is now $357 .80 for a total of $1,571.36 for no added advantage.

By exploring different options and routes, I was able to drop an initial $1,806.56 trip down to $1,518.56 saving $288. On this trip, between Orbucks and Bank of America, I would earn $38 toward hotel stays which effectively drops the plane ticket under $1,500.

It pays to look at alternative ways to book. Be flexible, save money.

$$

Flexibility in dates in dates can also save a lot of money. Many airfare booking Websites allow you the opportunity to checkout fares +/- 3 days of a chosen date, which is great if you have a narrow range of travel, but if you are open to a larger array of dates, you may very well find a greater range in pricing to match.

I found the two best deals I have ever had flying while not looking for a flight and not planning a trip. It was Monday, September 7, 2015, Labor Day, and I was online doing other things when I saw an ad for steep Labor Day discounts with Spirit Airlines.

Their deal required the use of a discount code that needed to be used for the reduced pricing by midnight that day. The booking had to be for flights in October or November. Some of the pricing was really remarkable.

I love to travel and I love to save money, so my time online suddenly changed. Where could I go? What could I see?

Spirit is one of the, if not the, largest discount carriers. One of their main bargains is their Bare Fare that includes nothing but the flight. This is straight from their Website, www.spirit.com:

> "BARE FARE™ *Our fares are fully unbundled. No 'free' bag. No 'free' drink. Other airlines bake those options right into their ticket price. We don't. A ticket with us gets you and a personal item from A to B.*"

So what kind of pricing can you get when one of the cheapest airlines offers huge discounts and *you don't care where you are flying to?*

I ended up booking two flights that day and the combined price was cheaper than any other airline ticket I have ever bought.

The first ticket was for a flight from Baltimore, MD to Dallas/Ft. Worth, TX for $68.18 — roundtrip. The second flight was for a trip from Baltimore, MD to Minneapolis/St. Paul, MN which was also $68.18 for the roundtrip ticket. I could not believe my luck in scoring two round trip airfares, that both crossed half the country, for only $136.16.

I remember arriving at the airport and the TSA agent asking if I was traveling for business or pleasure. I said pleasure. She looked at the ticket and questioned, "Minneapolis? I thought you were going on vacation. I was expecting to see the Caribbean. What's worth seeing in Minneapolis?" I simply replied, "A lot!"

It is that kind of thinking that adds to the expenses of vacationing. Not every great vacation needs a glamorous beach or exotic city. Having been to all 50 states nearly twice now, I assure you there is plenty to see in and do in the "not as popular" places to go.

The truth is that trip to Minneapolis was going to be very little about exploring that city. I had been there before and I was using it merely as a jumping off point for my explorations. My first real destination was the Apostle Islands National Lakeshore. It is one of our truly awe-inspiring National Parks and there is a good chance you never heard of it. Give it a Google and see how incredibly beautiful it is. I probably would have never found out about if I hadn't explored where a $68 plane ticket would get me.

Beyond saving money on plane tickets, another huge benefit to exploring places off the beaten path is everything tends to be more affordable (car rentals, hotels, food, etc).

Living in the Caribbean, I miss the opportunity for low-cost flights. Unfortunately every flight out of here is expensive, but it is the price you pay living where other people like to vacation.

The next time you are planning a vacation, why not see where you can get the cheapest flight and plan from there? You never know what you will end up seeing.

$$

My last tip of advice for plane travel is to avoid checking a bag at all cost. With a standard carry-on bag and a back pack, I have managed to get by even on some longer trips. Besides saving the fees associated with checked bags, it also saves a lot of time at the airport as you do not have to stand around watching the baggage carousel. This is a huge time saver on international flights as you can get closer to the front of the line at customs as you are far ahead of the rest of the plane waiting for bags.

Having fewer bags also makes customs go much faster and you also often do not have to check-in at your airline counter when first arrive at the airport. When possible, I print my boarding pass at home and head straight to security.

I managed to use carry-on only for a 12-day trip to Alaska and Hawaii — two very different climates. My wife and I used carry-on only for a 2-week trip through South America and another 2-weeker through Italy and Switzerland. We still had plenty of room for souvenirs.

Pack light, pack tight to save time and money.

$$

After scoring your best deal on a flight or deciding on a road trip, the next step in traveling is figuring out where you will be sleeping. Accommodations can get pricey, especially if you want more and more luxuries.

Let's start at the bottom of the barrel: sleeping in your car. Yes, it provides shelter, but it also offers a lack of comfort, questionable security, and a no bathroom option.

When I did my 50-state challenge I did have one evening that I had to resort to crashing in my car due to the poor assumption I would be able to find an affordable hotel in a specific area of Vermont. I spent the night parked in a highway rest area so I at least had a toilet, but no shower. You can safely assume that I do not recommend this.

Camping is often a cheap option for an overnight. There are plenty of parks that offer a ton of options for tent camping and many have toilets and showers. I only consider camping if I am on a road trip as camping gear adds too much to take onto a plane.

I have yet to explore using hostels, although I know many travelers that happily use them. They are also a very inexpensive and convenient way to travel.

My two favorite options for inexpensive accommodations are CouchSurfing.com and Airbnb.com.

I found out about "Couch Surfing" when I was running the 50 states. This Website was crucial in allowing me to reach my goal as I would have been buried in accommodations costs.

Couch Surfing harkens back to the day of the weary traveler coming into town who needs a safe place to lay their head down for the night (or two or three). The Website allows travelers (Surfers) to reach out to others online that have offered to host them at no cost. This service is worldwide.

As the name implies, sometimes you are just sleeping on a couch but that is not always the case. I have personally surfed in over 50 homes and have slept on couches, in my own private room, a personal suite, and even an entire apartment. Three times I have stayed in people's homes that were not even there — they either left me a key or left the door unlocked for me.

I have Couch Surfed in 33 states and even used the site for one free night on Easter Island.

I finished my 50-sate challenge with a 12-day trip to Alaska and Hawaii. That entire trip was Couch Surfed including 7 days driving around the Big Island of Hawaii. Imagine spending 7 nights in Hawaii with zero hotel costs. The savings was wonderful, but the people were amazing.

I originally found Couch Surfing because of the need to find cheap accommodations, but I have stayed an active Couch Surfer because the community is amazing. I am also a host now so I can "pay back" the community.

It is a terrific way to meet like-minded individuals that love traveling. I have stayed in touch with many of the people that I have met through Couch Surfing. Several have hosted me a second (or even third) time. Some have revisited their stays with me and a few I have even traveled with on other trips.

It is a truly fascinating community and I strongly encourage you to check it out.

The other Website I use, Airbnb.com, allows travelers to find rooms, homes, or whatever else private individuals want to offer up for rent in the way of accommodations. That said, the spaces are not free.

Through that site I have rented private rooms, complete apartments, full houses, travel campers, and even one night in a tipi. Like Couch Surfing, Airbnb is worldwide. I have rented through Airbnb in 15 countries so far and have several more booked.

Since you are renting space from private individuals, it is often much cheaper than a hotel or you get significantly more options than you would at hotel. My wife and I tend to book entire homes or apartments which always have full kitchens.

One of the most terrific aspects of Airbnb is that you genuinely get to live like a local as you have keys to your own private apartment in your new neighborhood. We have had rented apartments in London, Paris, Rome, Milan, Florence, Naples, and Zurich. Staying in your own apartment gives a much more insightful feeling to our trips than staying at cookie-cutter hotels.

There are times that hotels or motels make more sense. They are convenient with 24-hour check in. With Airbnb and Couch Surfing, you will probably be a bit of an imposition checking in late.

As mentioned earlier, when I book travel through Orbitz I rack up Orbucks toward hotel stays so when I do need a hotel, I rarely pay full price — if anything at all.

$$

My wife and I did a 32-day road trip around the U.S. Actually, we were not married at the time, but spending more than a month in a rental car went a long way toward convincing me to marry her.

She had never used CouchSurfing or Airbnb before. She had never camped either. Throughout our month on the road, we mixed up accommodations between those three options and some nights staying with friends or in hotels. Our average cost for nightly accommodations on that trip was $38.

As stated at the beginning of this chapter, there can be a big price tag on travel or maybe there isn't. It really depends on when, where, and how you want to travel.

Chapter 10

Negotiating: Know the Value
Large Expenses

Many people do not enjoy negotiating, haggling, bargaining, or whatever you want to call it. I'm not one of those people.

Well, sort of.

My stance on haggling is I don't do it — at least not how most people do. Most people thinking of negotiating price as this back-and-forth, tug of war to see where the final *price* falls.

I don't do that. I *evaluate* the item in question and decide on it's *value*. Once I am comfortable with my *valuation*, I set my figure. At that point, I share that figure and that is that. It is either accepted or it's not.

To sum up my negotiating steps:
Step 1: Determine value (*not price*).
Step 2: Walk away if the value is not agreed upon.

My philosophy is this: The strongest hand you can have in any negotiation is to know the value and be willingly to walk away from the deal if your target is not met. The key is to not want something so badly that you can't walk away from it.

$$

Let me illustrate this with a two examples: Car purchase and a property investment.

In the fall of 2007 I cashed out of Jekyl Hyde Racing — sold everything. Since that included all cars associated with the racing business, I needed to buy another car for daily driving.

I knew I still wanted a nice car, which had some level of performance, but also some level of luxury. I had spent over a decade in small sports cars and I was ready for some comfort. After years of racing, I had enough with shifting gears and wanted an automatic.

After doing my homework, I had my sights set on a 2000-2004 BMW, either a 3 or 5 series, and preferably in silver. They made a ton of these cars and they were readily available on the used market; however, their conditions were all over the place. Some of the cars were unbelievably beat up. Some were decent, but priced extremely high.

My search area was within a 2 hour radius of my home and I spent a lot of time looking at cars. One night I saw a gorgeous 2001 BMW 528i for sale at a Volvo dealership near Philadelphia which was stretching my two-hour drive time. It was listed at $13,900.

My girlfriend and I made the drive after work and we really needed to make time to get there well before closing time for the dealership, so there was no stopping for dinner. I am someone who gets hangry so the lack of food was potentially going to be a factor for me.

The dealership knew we were coming and had the car sitting out front, freshly cleaned, and waiting for us. After exchanging pleasantries with the salesman, we went for a test drive. It was the cleanest and smoothest used BMW I had driven and I had driven more than two dozen during my search.

I asked the salesman to confirm the price and he said it was $13,900, but he was sure they could let it go for $13,500. Terrific, I am $400 to the good on the *price* and I haven't even talked about the *value* at this point.

The price was well above the other cars I had driven, but this was in better condition. The salesman assured me they had a clean Carfax for the car and it only had one previous owner who recently traded it in on a new Volvo. It had just about 70K miles which is right about where I prefer a used car to be.

I told him I was interested in buying the car and he said wonderful while inviting me into the office. We sat down at his desk and I explained that I was very interested in buying the car, but I did not value the car as high as $13,500.

He asked me what sort of monthly payment I was looking to pay. This is a common tactic; they always want to nail a monthly payment to your budget instead debating the actual value of the car. On that logic, you could finance a Lamborghini for 30 years and have a $300 per month car payment, but what do you think you would end up paying in interest? I kindly explained that I was not interested in talking about the monthly payments; I wanted to discuss the *value* of the car.

He asked me to hold on for a moment while he went to talk to the sales manager. This is typical car dealership sales tactics. They go back and forth between the salesperson and the manager trying to work out an amazing deal just for you!

The salesman returned triumphantly announced that since we drove so far and it was the end of the month, etc. that the manager said he could sell the car for $12,800.

We were now down $1,100 from the original asking *price* and I had yet to share where I *valued* the car.

I told him that I appreciate him talking to the sales manager, but that was not where I *valued* the car. He pulled out his calculator, punched in a bunch of numbers, and pointed out that at $12,800 the monthly payments would only be _____. I don't recall the figure as this did not matter to me. Once again, I politely explained that I was not interested in talking about monthly payments, but the *value* of the car.

He finally asked, me what I was looking to pay. I said, "I *value* the car at $12,500."

He attacked his calculator again and said that is only a $10 difference in a monthly payment. I explained that I was talking about the *value* of the car and I was not interested in talking about payments. I further pointed out that I when I said $12,500, I meant *all-inclusive* at $12,500.

He asked what I meant and I said I was willing to pay $12,500 for the car including the taxes, tags, and registration. Clearly frustrated, he started tapping on the calculator and, with attitude, said, "That puts the price of the car down to $11,600."

I said, "Okay."

He said, "That's not going to happen. It's over $2,000 off the price of the car."

I said, "Ok, but that is where I value the car. It looks like we came close, but we obviously don't have a deal. Thank you."

This is when things turned unfortunate.

The salesman sat back smug in his chair and announced, "I see what's going on here. You have bad credit and are only pre-approved for $12,500. That is why you are so firm."

Later on, my girlfriend explained to me that my chair actually shot backward because I stood up so quickly as I said, "No, you have it wrong. I do not have poor credit. In fact, I have nearly perfect credit. I was discussing the value of the car, not the payments, because I am a cash buyer. I know the *value* of the car. There was no reason to insult your customer like that."

I walked out of the dealership and got into our car. My girlfriend followed, got in, and asked, "What just happened? Did he just insult you?"

We left and stopped for fast food two blocks down the street. I called a BMW mechanic I know and told him about the car. He asked a couple of key questions about the car and pointed out that I was actually looking at a highly upgraded "sport" edition of the 5 series that was worth several thousand dollars more than I had originally thought! We chuckled at my firm price on a car that was better than I (or the salesman) realized.

As we finished our fast food, my phone rang. It was the dealership. I heard the salesman saying, "Mr. Fazio after you left the sales manager asked what happened. When I explained it to him, he insisted that I call to apologize. I am sorry and I did not mean to insult you. Being so close to the city, we get a lot of people with poor credit. I realize you are probably no longer interested in the car, but the sales manager said if you are willing to come back, we can let it go for $12,500 — all inclusive."

I thanked him for the call and the apology. I indicated that we were already a good way home, but give us a minute to discuss it. I told my girlfriend what just transpired and she asked if I was going to go back and buy it. I said that I would.

I called the salesman back and thanked him again for the apology and the offer to sell the car at $12,500. I went onto to explain that we would have to drive all the way back to the dealership and then still had a two-plus hour drive home. I said I noticed the car only had a ¼ tank of gas when we test drove it and we would be willing to come back and buy it at $12,500 if it also had a full tank of gas. At this hour, we didn't want to have to stop on the way home.

He agreed.

We waited a while and drove the 2 blocks back to the dealership and bought the car, with a new washing and full tank of gas, for $12,500 all inclusive.

Having looked at many of these cars, I knew where I *valued* the automobile and I was, most importantly, willing to walk away from the deal.

$$

I mentioned earlier that after a starting a new job in the fall of 2011, I went looking for a two- or three-unit investment property in the city near my new position. My Realtor was fantastic and showed me plenty of properties.

Early in our search, on Friday, August 26 we looked at three properties, one of which I really liked. It was a two-unit building with a solid, long-term tenant upstairs and a month-to-month tenant downstairs. The neighborhood was in the city, but a very quiet street across from a park with a small lake. It was by far the best property that we had looked at in my price range ($70,000 – $100,000).

My Realtor and I finished looking through the place and we were standing on the side porch, looking toward the back yard. There was a giant tree about halfway back and one large limb was arched downward toward the roof. It was just barely touching the building. We both eyed it and my Realtor said, "If you buy this one, you are going to have to get that tree trimmed back."

I sent him a message on Saturday letting him know that I wanted to make an offer on the building. He said he would contact the selling agent and get back to me.

Over the weekend Hurricane Irene came through Pennsylvania wreaking all sorts of havoc.

Ray, my Realtor, called me on Monday. He said the selling agent got back to him and that he was sure we wouldn't want that property any more. When I asked why, he reminded me about that tree. He said it did not survive the hurricane. It had split in two and severely damaged the building. I couldn't believe it.

I drove by after and, sure enough, when the tree split a large portion bounced off the roof of the building and then hit the covered brick side porch we had been standing on. The other part of the tree went the other direction taking out the neighbor's fence, bouncing off their roof, and landing on their garage.

The place was off the list. Ray and I went back to searching. I have no idea how many properties Ray showed me over the next 2 months, but none of them were quite right. It was so hard having seen a really "good one."

At some point in our search, I told Ray the story of my BMW purchase. He got a chuckle out of the "hard ball" with the salesman and that I finally got to pay precisely what I *valued* the car at.

By the end of October Ray called me and said that the selling agent from that first building called and let him know that all of the damage had been repaired and that the selling *price* came down. We decided to go back and have another look.

The work that was done was done very well and the place looked great. I told Ray that I wanted to make an offer.

The original asking price for the place was $116,000, but it had sat on the market for nearly a year. When we first looked the place, pre-hurricane, it had been marked down to $100,000 which seemed on the high end of the range compared to other places we had looked at.

After the work was done, the Realtor called and said the new price was $96K. Ray asked me what I wanted to offer.

I said I felt the place was worth $80,000. Ray said, "Ok, but what do you want to offer?"

I replied, "$80,000. That's what I am willing pay."

Ray said that was not giving me any negotiating room. I reminded him that I do not negotiate. He laughed and asked if I mind if he negotiates.

I told him to do whatever makes him happy, but I wasn't *valuing* the place any more than $80K. Ray said fine and that he would offer $78K.

A few days later Ray got back to me. He said the sellers, through their Realtor, said that if all they were going to get was lowball offers then they would keep the place as a rental and keep collecting the income, but since it had been on the market for a while, they were willing to let it go for $92,000.

I told him that I was still feeling that $80K was the right figure and he took that back to the selling agent. A couple more days passed and Ray called. He was ecstatic as they countered at $84K and felt this was a really great price. He was pleased that they dropped so much. He asked me what my response would be to the new offer.

I said, "$80,000."

Ray said, "You have to be kidding. You are going to lose this place over $4,000?" I said no, I am only going to pay what I felt the place was worth and that was $80,000.

I felt bad for him and I could hear the frustration as we had put a lot of time into this search and Ray had done a phenomenal job, but I had my eye on the big picture.

Besides truly feeling the place was worth $80,000 based on looking at a ton of properties, I also had a keen understanding of the seller's position. Over the months I had learned they recently had completed a divorce and this was their last asset to split.

The place had been on the market for over a year. Winter was getting ready to roll in and they would have to cover the high heating bill for the tenants. They had also just got done wading through the nightmare of insurance and repairs from Hurricane Irene. I was certain they were itching to unload the place.

Lastly, for a multi-unit building in Pennsylvania, you had to have 25% to put down. How many potential buyers had solid credit, pre-approval above the negotiated price, and $20,000 to put down?

I told Ray, "Please tell them that I said thank you for considering my offer and that I wish them well with their sale."

Ray sighed and said, "Okay."

Two weeks later, around 8:00 p.m. on a Friday night, I was at dinner with students I had taken away on a weekend road trip when my phone rang. It was Ray.

I answered it and heard Ray say, "I can't believe it. The selling agent just called and asked if the $80,000 offer was still on the table. It's just like the story you told me with the BMW."

Ray asked for my response, and I replied, "Tell them the $80K offer is still on the table and they have the sale as long as they pick up the tab on the home warranty."

Most properties in my area have the option to buy a home warranty for around $400 that covers issues you might have in the first year. They accepted this final offer and I took the keys to my first intentionally bought investment property.

Incidentally, I used that warranty twice to cover appliances that would have cost me several hundred dollars to repair.

In the end, I was able to purchase the place for exactly what I *valued* it at. It is also worth noting that in order to get a mortgage a property must get an assessment done. The assessed *value* came back at precisely $80,000.

$$

Knowing how much you *value* a purchase, makes it easier to settle on what *price* you are willing to pay. It literally takes the haggling out of one side of the equation. Once you set your mind on a *value*, it's really up to the other person to haggle with the situation until the reach your number or the deal goes bust.

For this to work, you have to be comfortable with letting the deal go bust. Being willing to walk away from a transaction — not wanting the 'thing' too much — gives all of the power of negotiation to you. When we come together for a purchase it is truly a battle of the 'wants.'

You want the item and they want your money. Who wants it more? This is why you never walk into a car dealership (or any other potential large purchase) and exclaim, "Oh my God! I want it! I have to have it!!" The ability to negotiate *price* just left the building.

It's better to seem interested, intrigued, or curious. Let them know they got your attention, but you are not sold. Let them make it more tempting. Whomever wants it more loses the bargaining power.

Try this simple test. Offer a realistic *value* to any street vendor, anywhere in the world and see it get rejected. Then see what happens when you walk away. Who wanted it more?

Chapter 11

Bad Habits
Choices that Cost

Habits are routines of behavior that you may or may not be aware that you are doing. Habits can be good and they can be bad. This chapter tackles my top 10 list of bad financial habits that I have done myself or witnessed in others. So much havoc is wreaked on people's finances by their own behavior and it often goes unnoticed.

If you can see yourself or your thinking in these bad habits, the hope is that reading about them will bring them to the forefront of your thinking so you are more aware. Having this awareness and identifying potential problems will be an important first step in correcting them.

$$

1. Getting used to a level of credit card debt

Although it has been 19 years since my personal bankruptcy, I can still clearly recall the mindset that I had lived under for years. I was 24 years old and I had been using — nay, abusing — credit cards since I was 18 years old.

I was working in restaurants full-time since I was 16 years old and had no problem establishing credit in my own name. I bought my first brand-new car when I was 17 and that opened the door to establishing credit.

As a college student working full-time and going to school to learn business management, I was not worried about money. I knew I would get my degree and a killer job with a big salary. Who cared how much credit card debt I racked up? It would get paid eventually.

Like many students, I changed majors and switched schools. I left the world of business management for the world of fine art. That move prolonged college, increased my student loan debt, and gave me several more years to intensify my credit card debts.

At my worst, I estimate I had 4 or 5 major credit cards and 3 or 4 store credit cards. The major cards all had many thousands of dollars on them. When I filed for bankruptcy the month before my 25th birthday, there was over $40,000 in credit card and personal loan debt.

The personal loan was used to buy a sports car that ultimately I wrecked without collision insurance. I was making payments on a car I no longer had. I did not have transportation and no lender was going to extend credit to me to buy another car. I was done. Bankruptcy was the only way out of the hole that I was starting to bury myself in.

How does one get so far into that abyss? One huge mistake I made is I got comfortable with a certain level debt. I didn't even blink when I opened up a monthly credit card statement with a $7,000 balance. Really the only thing that caught my eye was the ever-increasing "minimum payment."

As life happens, sometime you come into a little bit of money and it offers you the chance to get ahead. Maybe you earn an extra $500 one month so, being a responsible adult, you put that toward your credit card bill.

You know what happens next? You get your next monthly statement and the balance is down to $6,500 instead of $7,000 and you start to think about what you can buy. Right?

Realistically, last month the bill was $7,000 and everything turned out fine. Surely that means you are okay to spend another $500 without worries. You will just be back where you were a month ago.

I remember that logic. I remember looking for something for $500 to buy even though I didn't actually need or want anything. I had the credit available, I was comfortable with seeing the level of debt so I just kept shopping, and shopping — swiping and swiping.

If you can even remotely see yourself, or part of your current financial thinking, in this scenario then you are headed down a very long and potentially dark path.

There is no good credit card debt — none. There is good debt out there and we will discuss that later, but for now, know that there is no good credit card debt.

Yes, I live religiously off my credit cards, but I carry no debt. I charge and pay it off every month. I have not paid a penny in credit card interest since my bankruptcy in 1998.

Do not get "used to" credit card debt. You might as well get used to quick sand. You have just as much chance of getting out of it.

If you have credit card debt, today is the day to stop. It is time to bring out a calculator, build a budget, and make a plan that you can reasonably stay focused on to get rid of that debt. Of all the debts you might have, credit is the one you must focus on relieving.

$$

2. Spending more because your debt feels hopeless

Just like we can get used to a certain level of debt, we can also get used to having debt in general. It rarely occurs to people in deep debt that it is not the natural state of things. It is easy to assume that everyone else is in just as much debt as you are.

The danger of getting used to debt and feeling that monthly pressure is that it is easy feel that you are permanently screwed and you will never get out of the hole. The next step in that reasoning is, "Well then it doesn't matter how big the hole is."

As Will Rogers famously said, "If you find yourself in a hole, stop digging."

I remember that feeling too. A major credit card would get maxed out at $4,000 and I would open up a new card with a higher limit and transfer the balance over. That did three, very bad things for me.

One, it obviously gave me a higher credit line on the new card. That meant I had so much more room to go shopping.

Two, it freed up the card I just paid off. That card with the $4,000 limit was wide open and ready to use!

Lastly, it started teaching me the losing game of balance transfer. How great did it feel completely payoff a credit card with a high balance? I felt like a rock star and under that positive feeling was the thought that I also did not need to make a minimum payment that month. It was not part of my realization the amount of interest that accrued that month and the next, and the next.

Having debt, especially bad debt, is not *natural*.

Just like my advice on getting used to a certain level of credit card debt, do not get used to having debt in general. Living a debt-free, or nearly debt-free, life is incredibly enjoyable and less stressful than seeing a pile of mail each month with impossible-to-pay amounts due.

$$

3. Assuming you will always have a payment

Earlier I spoke about my coworker Kevin that always had to have the latest video game the day it came out. Actually, the need to have something the moment it is released could probably be on this list as we often pay a premium for the latest shiny object. We will not add that bad habit into this list, but take that under advisement too.

Let's get back to Kevin. In the eight years I worked with Kevin, I am not sure how many cars he purchased. It was at least, maybe three. His car purchases were always a point of concern for me because he always rolled over the debt from the previous car into the new car.

Dealerships are great at helping you do this. Bring your trade in and we will get you into a new car — regardless of what you owe. It sounds enticing and it is. The reality is that you will, one way or another, pay for the car that you did not finish making payments on. All the dealership does is roll it into one bigger loan.

I tried talking to Kevin about this and he said he wasn't worried. He said it would never matter how much he owed. When I asked him why not, he simply replied, "I'll just always have a car and car payment. It's just one of those bills."

When I tried to explain the intricacies of how much he would be paying for all of these cars he said all that mattered is that the monthly payment was affordable. He had accepted the reality of this omnipresent bill.

The alternate viewpoint of paying off a car and actually owning it was of no interest. I am sure at this point he has paid a ton in interest. I haven't spoken to Kevin in a decade. I can only guess what he is driving and how much of a loan he is paying on for it. I would hope that somewhere along the way he was able to alter his thinking and get ahead on paying off a car.

I don't even want to think about the possibility that he ever totaled a car and had to deal with an insurance company only offering him what the current car was worth, not the bundle of cars he had wrapped into a singular loan. There are so many ways that rolling over debt can catch up with us.

I try to run my personal finances like a business. If I can eliminate a bill, that frees up monthly cash flow for something else. I always have my focus on which bill I can eliminate.

Don't assume that you always will have a certain type of bill. If you look to eradicate certain bills from your life, you will be amazed at what you can accomplish and how much extra money you have each month.

$$

4. Spending more when you make more

I mentioned before about getting a new job that was an hour away and that is when I started looked to buy a two-unit investment building. At the time, I wasn't planning on living there full time. My plan was to stay there several nights per week.

With the tenant paying the mortgage and most of the utilities, I would have a place to stay whenever I needed it for the price of my utilities and some other, nominal costs. All of my costs would mostly be covered by the money I would save in gas and wear-and-tear on my car.

At the time I got that job and was devising this plan, I was driving the BMW I hard-bargained for in the last chapter. Although I loved the car, I had no interest in putting a ton of miles on it commuting. I was also not interested in spending over an hour every day in traffic — even more in the winter when it snowed.

I set my plan in motion and started looking for that investment. The night I settled on the place I was going to buy and was preparing to make the offer, I ended up on the phone with my brother. I excitedly explained my plans to him.

He said there was no need to buy another property. Why take the risk? He said, "You have a new job and are making good money. Treat yourself. Buy one of the new Fiats that you really like."

He rationalized that the Fiat would be much better on gas than the BMW, which was true. He said I had earned it and deserved it, to which I also would agree.

This "logic" is what many people succumb to as they get promotions or get better jobs with increased salaries. Unfortunately, this new-found wealth gets eaten up by the new-found spending. Just because you make more does not mean that you have to spend more.

I ended up being at that job for four years. Let's play out how those four years would have looked if I had purchased the new Fiat with all of the options I would have preferred. The price of the car would have been roughly $20,000. That happened to be as much cash as I had available that I was willing to part with.

The moment I bought the car, it would have immediately lost value — roughly $2,000. Then, I would have spent 4 years driving 100 miles roundtrip to work every day.

Factoring in four weeks of vacation, the car would have been driven for 48 weeks, or 240 days. The total miles put on the car, just for driving back-and-forth to work, would have been 24,000 per year for a total of 96,000 miles! Imagine that. In four years' time a brand new car might be clocking 100,000 on the odometer and that is not counting personal miles driven.

We haven't even factored in the negative financial effects of winter driving, lost time and stress on the commute, wear-and-tear on the car, and the need to have oil changes every month and a half.

What would that car be worth after those four years?

What about the time lost? In those four years, I would have spent 20 days commuting and that assumes 24 hours of non-stop driving. If you only consider a normal work day of eight hours, it would have been the equivalent of 60 days of "work" doing the commute over four years. Who wants to spend their life like that?

On the positive side, I would have improved gas mileage from roughly 22 mpg in the BMW to 30 mpg in the Fiat. The BMW would have required roughly 4,364 gallons of fuel versus 3,200 gallons to run the Fiat. At a cost of $2.60 per gallon of fuel, the Fiat would have saved me $3,026.40.

After four years, my $20,000 car might now be worth $11,000. I lost $9,000 in net worth and 60 days of my life driving. We can add back in the $3,000 saved in fuel, but we also have to add in a ton of driving stress.

Now, let's compare that to the purchase of the building I bought. I put my $20,000 down on the building which immediately gave me equity, better interest rates, and no need to pay for private mortgage insurance (PMI). That equity is mine, and as long as something unusual did not happen to negatively affect the value of the property, that equity value should grow.

I now lived less than 2 miles from work which was close enough that I could get there in a five-minute drive or a 10-minute bicycle ride. I rode the bicycle as often as I could, which increased my health and eliminated all commuting stress — even that from a five-minute drive. When I saw traffic jams, I simply rode past them.

My overall housing costs were much less than where I was living 50 miles away so I also enjoyed substantial savings every month on bills. When you factor in the tenant that was paying rent that covered almost the entire mortgage, the net worth was growing every month — not losing value as it would have with the new Fiat purchase.

I bought the building for $80,000 and after four years of ownership, I managed to sell it for $94,500.

With the building purchase, I was able to add on roughly $15,000 to my net worth instead of losing nearly $9,000.

Given the same choice, would you rather earn $15,000 or lose $9,000 for the sake of having a brand new car? People who purchase new cars pay an extreme premium for that new car scent.

Keep in mind, that in this scenario, the new car was purchased with cash — not a loan. With reasonable credit and $2,000 down on the new car, it would have cost an additional $1,200 in interest payments.

Another factor worth considering is what would have happened if two years into either plan I lost my new, higher-paying job? I would have potentially had the choice of selling the car at a loss or cashing out the equity in the building. Having the equity would have provided me options. Having the commitment of a car loan would have provided a lot of stress.

Sadly, I witnessed this scenario play out for many of my colleagues at that new job. We went through many rounds of layoffs over the four years I was there. With each round there were depressing stories of colleagues that could no longer afford their new homes or fancy cars. Every time I saw this happen, I was grateful that if I lost my job I had a tenant paying most of my bills and that I was living well below my means. It provided an enormous amount of security going through the hell of layoffs.

It is easy to fall into the financial trap of "I am making more money so I can spend more." My thinking for the last 20 years has been the exact opposite. Every time I make a significant jump up in income, I look harder for ways to save money. My feeling is that when I make more money, and cut more costs, then my available cash for spending (or better yet, investing) will be greater.

How often do we see friends or family members get that new job or promotion and they immediately look for a newer car or bigger house? Maybe it's new furniture or a new wardrobe.

Think of it this way. If you feel broke all the time while you are making $2,000 per month and spending $2,000 per month; then, you will feel just as broke making $3,000 and spending $3,000. In fact, it might actually feel worse, because logically you know you are making more money, but can't figure out why you are not getting ahead.

I feel like sometimes people are not comfortable with having an excess cash flow. The idea of having more money than you need seems foreign to some; therefore, every dollar earned needs to find a way to be spent. If only people would spend less as they made more, there would be significantly less stress in the world.

At the very least, when your income goes up, if you do not change anything, you will increase your potential saving and investing. It is much better to live a $40,000 per year life style on a $60,000 per year salary than it is to live the $60,000 lifestyle on the $60,000 income.

If you followed the earlier advice of living below your means, then you may have been living a $30,000 lifestyle on a $40,000 income. If you maintain that lifestyle at a $60,000 income, then you can save/invest almost half of your earnings!

$$

5. Accepting unhealthy addictions

All throughout college I drove sports cars. I was one of those guys that defined themselves by what he drove and what I drove had to have two seats and a ton of performance. One day I pulled up to class and managed to grab one of the coveted spots in front of our academic building.

I noticed that as I pulled up one of my classmates was standing outside smoking. Even though he sat behind me, we had never exchanged a single word. He was just one of those guys that you recognize from around, and you hear him talking every day behind you, but there was never a reason or interest in getting to know him.

This particular day, I could feel his eyes watching me pull up, park, and get out of my car. My car had T-tops; removable pieces of glass that offered a convertible-type feel. As I installed the glass roof panels, I was aware that he was still staring as he puffed away.

A few minutes later he came into class and sat in his usual seat behind me. I was talking to a good friend of mine, sitting next to me, when I heard this guy behind me say, in an intentionally loud voice, "I don't understand how some guys in college can afford a sports car."

Without skipping a beat, I said to my friend in a similarly loud voice, "I don't understand how some guys in college can afford to drink every night."

I did not get to see his reaction and we finished the semester without ever exchanging words directly on any subject whatsoever. The reality is, we were both making observations and comments on each other's addictions.

He was the dude that spent all of his money on alcohol and cigarettes. I was the guy who spent all of my money on sports cars. We each had our addictions.

Addictions come in a large variety and they can often be destructive. My fascination with sports cars dominated my spending for years and greatly affected my financial well-being. It is possible that without my car addiction I may have avoided bankruptcy — maybe not. Maybe it just helped it come along that much quicker.

I don't know how my classmate managed in life, but it would not be hard to imagine what his nightly binge drinking may have cost him. Addictions can be unhealthy for many reasons and there are plenty of psychology books out there that can address this topic better than I ever could.

I'm not going to explore the psychology of addiction here. What is relevant to this book, is realizing the financial impact of addictions. More often than not, addictions cost money and if we can't control our addictions then we are most likely not controlling our spending either.

6. Bragging about what you spend, not what you save

Do you like to name drop the brands you purchase? If so, is that because you are interested in owning quality merchandise or because you enjoy the status? Maybe you like both. The real question is: Are you more likely to boast that you paid $300 for a Gucci watch or do you get more excited that you scored the identical watch for $150?

I see nothing wrong with enjoying quality merchandise and prefer one brand over another. The concern is if part of sharing your latest acquisition is how much you spent, rather than how much you saved.

The only people who are going to be impressed that you spent a lot of money on an item are the ones that are similarly willing to pay top dollar. I suspect that most people are more impressed if you found an amazing deal.

7. Making minimum payments

If you are only paying minimum payments on debts — especially credit cards — you are in for a rude math awakening. You might have better luck getting out of quicksand than credit card debt with minimum payments.

Let's look at an example to show how devastating minimum payments can be: You have a particularly bad month for unexpected expenses (refrigerator dies, car breaks down, etc.). You grab your trusted credit card as a quick fix to get you out of these surprise expenses.

A few swipes later, and all is well in the world. You love your new fridge, the car is running better than ever, and you are glad to have gotten through the worst of it — or have you?

Thirty days later your credit statement arrives with a new balance of $2,539.26! Whoa. Where are you going to find that kind of money? No worries. The minimum payment is *only* $51. You are going to be okay. Of course you can come up with $50.

Now, let's assume you do not ever charge anything on that credit card again until this debt is paid off. You are dedicated to this mission and vow to not add any more debt to this bill. With equal confidence, you also vow to religiously pay $51 per month until the debt is gone.

For this example, we are going to assume an annual percentage rate (APR) of 13.99% interest.

At that interest rate and a payment rate of $51 per month. It will take roughly six years — SIX YEARS — to pay off that $2,500 debt. Even worse is that you will have paid around $1,182.36 in interest. The actual interest paid is nearly half the original amount charged. That is equivalent to paying 50% more for every item you bought.

This scenario can actually get much worse than this. If instead of being committed to paying $51 per month, you decided to just keep paying the minimum payment; then you would be paying the debt off over a much longer time than six years and racking up significantly more in interest payments.

Why? Because as the balance gets lower, the credit card companies do you a "favor" and lower the minimum payment. Not surprisingly, they do not lower the interest rate. This is a way to milk you for more cash and keep their revenues growing.

The only way to win this game is to not play it at all. This is why I do not carry credit card debt. I pay the amount due in full every month.

If for some reason I could not afford to pay off all that I bought that month, I would make the largest possible payment and keep doing so until that balance was zero.

This logic applies to all other debts as well. Credit cards tend to be the worst debt as the interest rates tend to be significantly higher than on other borrowed amounts.

This reasoning is why I don't even pay my basic mortgage bill every month. I make sure I always add something else to the principal. Every single, extra dollar you put down toward the principal is another dollar you will never pay interest on again.

8. Living beyond means

This is by far one of the worst traps people put themselves into. They misuse credit, loans, and other financing to live the lifestyle they feel they *deserve* instead of the one they have *earned*.

Even if they aren't borrowing, they might be living paycheck to paycheck with nothing remaining after the check is spent. This is why millions of Americans are one, maybe two, paychecks away from financial catastrophe.

If you are holding your breath waiting for the next pay check to cover today's expenses, this might be you. It's easy to do. Our culture makes us feel that we need to have new cars, the latest cell phone, and the next amazing gadget, but the truth is we do not need any of these items.

For example, I'll share the story of the guy I bought my race car from. Well, it wasn't a race car when I bought it. It was just a decent sports car with a lot of potential. It was a 1991 model and I purchased it on December 1, 2001. At 10 years old, these cars were typically selling for $5,000–$12,000 depending on condition.

The particular car I was looking at had very high mileage and a dented fender. Even in that condition, it was for sale well below book value at $1,750.

When I showed up at the guy's house to look at the car, his place was amazing. It was this incredibly large, brand new home in a newly designed development. I am guessing it was a well-over $350,000 property.

In the driveway there were two brand-new cars and the older sports car I was looking at. We took the car for a drive and everything seemed in order. I was going to buy the car. When we got back to his house, he invited me in.

My jaws dropped as we walked into this immaculate home — it was completely empty. There was no furniture on the first floor except for one small, inexpensive table in the dining room.

He introduced me to his wife, who was clearly many months pregnant. He acknowledged the big baby bump and explained it was time to sell his toy — the sports car.

I was happy to buy the car, but I was completely blown away by the façade of the household. From the street, it looked like they had it made with several of the latest cars and a new home. The inside told a different story. Yes, there could be other explanations for their situation, but I was definitely left with the impression that they were stressed about money.

If so, how much could that stress have been reduced by a previously-owned home in a more modest neighborhood with a pair of certified pre-owned cars?

I worked for a newspaper for eight years photographing people's homes and so many times I got the impression that people were not really affording all that they had. I have seen this with my friends and family, and it was even me at one time.

Like any problem, the first step is acknowledging that you have one. If you are not budget savvy and are not confident in how you are paying your bills every month, then maybe you have bitten off more than you can chew.

If, after covering your monthly expenses, you do not have something left to save or invest, then you are probably living beyond your means.

9. Not investing money

These last two points are not really bad habits as they are behaviors that are detrimental by *not* doing them. I will include them here as they are still behaviors that negatively affect our ability to grow wealth.

When money is properly invested, it can work for you. It can make more of itself. How amazing is it that money can be self- replicating? It just has to be put in the right environment and many people do not take advantage of this.

I know too many people that have either not invested in their company's 401(k) retirement plans at all or have not explored the maximum potential in these plans by investing more.

What about the stock market? How many people do you know that currently have money directly invested in the stock market? The New York Stock Exchange often sounds like this big scary, dangerous beast that will swallow all of your money the moment you make your first investment. That is like saying that if you travel to NYC you will be robbed on the street the first day you get arrive.

Yes, people do get robbed their first day in NYC, but many millions more do not. It is about being smart and careful. Success in the stock market can be had with very basic investment techniques that do not require an investment degree.

We all define success differently. I do not mean to imply that with basic stock purchase you are going to suddenly make millions of dollars in the market. By success in the market, I mean (at a minimum) beating the returns from savings accounts or leaving your money in cash.

Leaving your money in cash, and even in many savings accounts, actually loses value over time due to inflation. Even most bank certificates of deposit (CD) that I have seen do not keep up with inflation.

If you are doing well with your budget and you have unallocated money left over after each pay check, then you need to put the money somewhere it will not lose value.

This does require some effort and some reading which I will get to in the #10 point of this section on bad habits. At this point, the realization needs to happen that the only thing that stops you from being an 'investor" is your mind set.

There are a number of online trading platforms that are reputable and very affordable to get started with buying stocks. If buying stocks directly is too intimidating, then look at buying mutual funds. Mutual funds are investment programs that are professionally managed and you can buy and sell share in them just a like a stock.

You will not have to search long or hard to find a mutual fund that offers significantly better returns than a bank savings account.

Another fear that people have with putting money in the stock market is that it seems like they will have limited access to the cash if it is needed for an emergency.

The trading company I used the longest was able to get me a check within a week of a stock sale. That is not as fast going to the bank and making a withdrawal, but the returns on my investment made this slight delay worthwhile.

Another huge area of life that people do not invest in is real estate. So many people rent, rather than own, and never realize the potential in building equity in their own lives. I have rented for more years than I have owned and I wish I could have seen the returns on investment that all of my landlords have seen on my monthly contributions to their net worth.

In fact, I am actually paying rent now as I am not ready to purchase property in the country I am currently living in, but I still own real estate in the United States and that adds to my net worth every month.

The title of "investor" is not reserved for people with special abilities, training, or knowledge. It's a title that should be shared by all of us. Don't let fear stop you from learning how to invest. Take small steps, see small gains, and build on what you learn.

10. Not learning about money

Unless you escape to the woods to live off the land; like it or not, money is an important part of life. Money is pivotal to our existence and being money smart is essential for maximizing success.

It is not hard to become money smart. It is just a matter of taking the time to read, learn, and ask questions. If this book is your first time reading about finances, then congratulations on taking your first step toward an improved financial life.

Whether this is your first book on money or your 15, it is still just one single book and will not answer everything there is to know about money, investing, finance, net worth, credit, etc. If you are devoted to consistently improving your financial health and well-being, then it is a life-long process of learning.

Not only do most people not read and learn about money, but they rarely even talk about it. When was the last time you talked to a co-worker, friend, or even a family member about investing?

It has been said that if you want to know where you will be in five years, ask yourself who are the five people you talk to most often and where will they be in five years? Wherever that is, it is probably where you will be.

If those five people use drugs often, within five years you are likely to be using drugs. If they go to church each week, you are more likely to end up being a church regularly. Add in any scenario, and this is probably true for you and the five people you most frequently interact with.

That said, if the five people you most often speak to are financially healthy, actively investing, and conscientiously budgeting their money while maintaining excellent credit and building net worth, then you are more likely to be doing well for yourself as well.

Twenty years ago I read nothing about money and my finances were a mess. I was bankrupt with a negative net worth. I made a change and actively engaged in the process of learning about finances. Now I am in a solid place financially with a near perfect credit score and an ever-increasing net worth selling out that million dollar value.

Where do you want to be in five years? 10? 25?

Chapter 12

Good Habits
Choices that Pay

This chapter will look at my top 10 list of good financial habits. The hope is you may start incorporating these ideas into your own life and make them a habit. I would suggest picking just a few to start with and turning them in to regular behaviors.

1. Calculating net worth

Do you know your net worth? Do you have a general idea of what it is? Do you at least have a hunch as to whether or not you are in positive territory?

It can be scary and humbling doing your fist net worth calculator, but it must be done. You need to know where you are now, at your starting point of a new financial future. So roll up the sleeves and start cranking on Excel. Throw in all of your assets and all of your liabilities (debts) and see where it shakes out.

Do not get down if you are not happy with the number. If you have not been monitoring your net worth, it is not unusual to be a bit surprised at how low the number might be.

Once you have that number, consider it Day 0. Start updating the calculator every month and watch it grow. If you watch it, it will grow. Just by the very nature of knowing you are measuring yourself every month, you will become much more cognizant of your spending. You will start to find creative ways to increase your net worth.

Remember, keeping an eye on your net worth tells you how much cash value you are retaining. Sometimes it is not how much, you make, but rather how much you keep.

2. Monitoring credit scores and reports

We talked about the importance of credit scores already and that your score indicates how well you are managing debt. It used to be challenging to get a copy of your actual credit scores, but many banks and credit cards are now offering the service for free. There really is no reason to not know your score anymore.

Credit scores are a performance number and performance numbers can be improved. Pay attention to how you use debt, especially credit cards. With any monthly payment, always make an effort to pay more than the minimum amount due.

Ideally you want to pay off entire credit card statements each month. If you can't pay it off entirely, then make the largest possible payments to keep the balance as low as possible. If you are carrying a balance, try not to add any new charges until the balance is resolved.

If you try to live "cashless," like I do and recommend, then it is possible that your monthly credit card statement shows a balance that is a high percentage of your available credit which can negatively affect your score. The goal here is not to build a history of having a large portion of your available credit used each month, even if you pay it off entirely.

So how do you make that number drop? You can request an increase in your credit available (if you are confident you will just not spend more). Another great idea is to make two payments each month instead of one.

The number that gets reported to the credit bureaus is your balance at the time the statement is issued. That said, if you have a credit card with a $3,000 limit and you charge $1,500 in a month, it will show up as 50% credit utilization. Ideally you want that number to be under $10–15%.

That said, go ahead and charge the $1,500 but make one payment of $1,200 before the statement is issued. That way the amount on your statement is only $300 which gets the credit utilization down to 10% ($300 of the available $3,000 credit available).

Along with monitoring your credit score, it is worth checking your actual credit report from time to time. This can be done for free through AnnualCreditReport.com every 12 months. You are allowed to get a free report from each credit bureau (Equifax, Experian and TransUnion). Even better, you can stagger the requests so that you get one report every 4 months to have an even better eye on your credit.

If you find errors on your report, dispute them. This can drastically help your credit score if resolved successfully. Do not dispute loans that you have paid off with on-time payments. A loan that has been successfully paid off in good standing helps your credit score. Leave it on there.

Make checking your credit score and your credit report a regular part of your routine — a habit — a good habit.

This is not something you want to wait until you are getting ready to make a large purchase like a house or a car. At that point, it might be too late to positively affect your score as it is this history that really matters.

3. Collecting coupons and noting sales

Although I was never a big coupon collector for weekly groceries, and I can't do it now as my current country of residence does not offer them, I have always looked out for big-ticket coupons. I appreciate the cost savings of 50 cents here or a dollar there, but I always felt that my time was worth more than the time to hunt for the smaller coupons.

That said, I had no issue using coupons that were readily available regardless of their value. I never hunted through the Sunday paper with a pair of scissors, but I have been known to skim through a grocery's circular before going down the first aisle.

I prefer the larger savings from electronics, airlines, or Websites that offer discount codes. They are also easier to find with quick searches online.

If you pay attention to the stores that you regularly shop at, you will notice the pattern of their sales. It does not take much effort to adjust your spending to ensure that your purchases line up with their sale's calendar.

With minimal effort, you can almost always get away from spending the suggested retail price on anything. Keep in mind that it is often not how much money you earn, but how much you manage to keep.

4. Minimizing expenses

Any good business person knows the benefits of reducing expenses and the positive effect on "the bottom line." When you are looking at the bottom-line figure, whether it is total income or net worth, reducing your expenses effectively (*and sometimes literally*) increase those numbers.

I mentioned earlier that in 1992 I got rid of cable television. I recently had turned 18 years old and had just moved into my first apartment. As any new tenant would do in 1992, I paid to turn on all of the necessary utilities: electric, phone (we still had landlines then), and cable. The water and trash were taken care of by the landlord.

At the time, I had just moved away from home to start my junior year of college. One afternoon I came back to my apartment, flopped on the couch, and turned on the television. With remote in hand, I started clicking, and clicking, and clicking.

The next memory I have of that day is it was nearly 11:00 p.m. and I had to get to bed. I was still clicking away when I realized the time. That night I accomplished nothing. I spent hours clicking away at the TV and never even watched a full show. I just kept clicking. I barely remember eating or using the restroom.

It really bothered me how quickly and easily I could throw away one of the greatest gifts we have — time.

I called the cable company the next day and requested they terminate my service. They questioned this as I had only had the service a month and they said I would have to pay to have the service uninstalled. I assured them that

I knew I wanted it turned it off and that it had already cost me too much.

That decision was nearly 26 years ago now. How much money have I saved since then by not having cable programming? I would estimate that I have saved at least $25,000.

How much is your cable bill? Take that amount and times it by 12 (months) and then by 26 (years).

We often do not think of our monthly bills in their total cost over a decade or two (or a lifetime). It is just too easy to pay an acceptable amount each month.

How much "life" have I gotten back by turning off the TV? This is a philosophical question and not one for a book on personal finance, but it is worth considering the added benefits of cutting expenses on things we may not really "need."

There is a whole host of other ways to cut expenses. Whenever I start a new job, I always consider housing options that will allow me to walk or bicycle to work instead of turning a car on and off every day. Like getting rid of cable television, this also gives me more "life" back as I tend to spend much less time commuting to work than most people.

When I travel, if there is a particular sight that I want to see, I will consider taking a taxi just one way and walking back or walking to the site and taking the taxi back. Not only does this save money and add exercise to my day, it also allows for serendipitous moments along the way that you would not have in a hired car.

There are always ways to cut expenses if you are willing to be creative and evaluate where your money is going.

One other example I will share is my choice of beverage at home. My fridge is usually stocked with Ocean Spray diet cranberry juices. They make a variety of flavors as they mix cranberry juice with mangoes, raspberries, grapes, etc.

I started drinking these because of the flavor and low calorie count (watching calories is a lot like watching finances). A few years ago I realized that I could save calories, and money, by mixing the juice with water.

When I finish a container of juice, I fill the empty container halfway up from a new juice bottle. I then top off both bottles with water. I effectively double my purchase for the same cost while slashing an already low calorie count in half.

Where can you cut expenses? How much can you save? What expenses do you have that you don't really "need?"

5. Taking advantage of loyalty programs

Whether it is the local coffee or sandwich shop that offers a return customer punch card or the local grocery that issues a rewards card, it pays to pay attention to loyalty programs. It is amazing how much money you can save with loyalty programs — especially with expensive items like airline tickets.

Every few months I enjoy something "free" from some business or another through loyalty programs. It really is worth your time to read and understand the programs offered from your favorite businesses.

6. Combining deals

Whenever possible, look for ways to combine promotions. If you are taking advantage of loyalty rewards from a particular business, pay attention to their regular sales and discounts. You will start to magnify your savings.

If you can, pay for these combined deals with a credit card that offers rewards. Do you recall the 37¢ Van Heusen shirt I bought by combining deals? That was included in a larger purchase of many items which I paid for on my Discover card so I ultimately got some of that money back!

7. Buying in bulk

There are several benefits to buying in bulk. Not only can you often swing a discounted price by buying a larger quantity, but you also reduce the number of trips (or shipping) that you pay for over time.

There is a very specific razor that I use and more than 10 years ago I found a seller on eBay that was moving large amounts of the razor for an unbelievable price *for that time.*

I bought so many razors under that pricing that I have not needed new razors in 10 years and I have enough stock to last a few years more. In that time, razors have significantly increased in price so my savings has been magnified over the years.

Because of the huge discounts some retailers offer on large quantities, they sometimes limit the number of items that can be purchased. Although you may be inhibited in how much you can buy at one location, many businesses have many locations and if the price is good enough, it may warrant driving around to another location (or two).

8. Buying used

People pay a very high premium for the new car smell or to be the first one to unwrap the plastic covering on a new gadget. So much money can be saved buying used, gently used items.

Earlier I spoke about a time when I had owned four cars: two 1991 Toyota MR2s, a 1998 Toyota MR2 and a 1987 Chevy Sprint. I purchased those four vehicles, used, for a total of $10,250. Around this time I started dating a recently divorced woman and, as part of her divorce, she acquired a brand-new 2004 Toyota Corolla for $14,000.

Within a year of us dating, I bought a fifth vehicle: a 1991 Chevy Suburban. This was bought to tow a trailer for one of the MR2s that was converted into a race car. I only paid $1,500 for that Suburban.

I was sitting on five vehicles that cost me a total of $11,750 to her one brand-new car for $14,000. Yes, her car was more reliable than any of the cars I had, but reliability is less of a concern when you have four or five cars at your disposal.

When it came time to sell the cars, I also retained a high resale value compared to initial purchase price as I did not immediately "lose money driving off the lot" like you do with a new car.

Around this time, people were spending $10-$20 on brand new DVDs. I was buying DVDs in bulk, used, for 10 for $25. As long as the disc is clean and plays, does it really matter if it is used? There are so many items in life that it simply does not make a significant, practical difference if an item is new or used — it is often a psychological difference. There is a pleasure in knowing you are the original owner, but at what cost?

What do you feel that you must buy brand new, but might be okay with a used version? There is money to be saved in buying used.

9. Learning about money

Whether this is the first book or the 50th book you have read on personal finances, keep reading. Financial acumen is like leadership and professionalism. They are areas that there is always room to grow no matter how much you have learned.

Do you know the difference between negative debt and positive debt? What about a Dividend Re-Investment Plan (DRIP)? What about the difference between a regular 401(k) and a Roth IRA? No? Then you have more reading to do. I am not getting into those topics here, but they are other important concepts for building wealth. Now you have something else to look up when you complete this book.

In addition to reading about finances, talk to people who know about money. If the five people you talk to most often are struggling financially and living paycheck to paycheck, then you most likely will too. Seek out people who are doing well and see what you can learn from them.

If you want to grow your net worth, improve your credit score, and increase your income, then surround yourself with others that have similar goals.

10. Making work optional

This is by far my favorite positive financial habit. Have you ever heard anyone talk about the size of their "FU Cash" what about their "KMA fund?" They are both referring to the same thing.

It is the sum of money needed to feel comfortable walking out of your job. How much would you need to have in readily available cash to not feel tied to your job? What kind of reserves would you want to have before telling your boss to "Fuck off" or "Kiss my ass?"

That amount of money is referred to as "FU cash" or a "KMA fund."

When I first heard about those phrases, I got to work building my reserves. I distinctly recall hitting my goal and having enough dollars saved that I did not feel handcuffed to my desk. It was an incredibly liberating feeling. It allows you to be much more confident at work.

I have since come to learn that there is something even more valuable that "FU cash." It is what I call "FU income." This is income that comes from sources other than the day job—ideally passive sources like rent or dividends. That money comes in whether or not you are working, sleeping, or traveling.

A funny thing happens when passive income, *FU income*, becomes greater than you monthly expenses. Work becomes optional.

Let that sink in for a moment.

If you can generate enough passive income to cover your monthly expenses, going to work becomes a choice.

I'm not there yet, but it is a goal I keep building toward. It is that type of planning and building that leads to early, enjoyable retirement.

Possessing those types of resources allowed me to not fear layoffs when they came around at my last employer. Many of my colleagues were devastated when they lost their positions. It was a significant financial burden. Over the course of 4 years I watched the pain of my coworkers as we went through 5 rounds of "reorganization."

On that 5th round, I was presented options of keeping parts of my job or taking a buyout. I eagerly accepted the buyout. There was reason to expect that the layoffs would continue for many more years (and they have) and I was in a financial position to embrace being unemployed.

Between my buyout, unemployment, and my passive income sources, I spent 6 months traveling and enjoyed a less-stressful job search. I am not aware of any of my counterparts being able to take advantage of the "opportunity" of being laid off.

Chapter 13

Buying Your Preferred Home for Free

Let's look at a scenario of a person that has $16,000 saved for a down payment for a home and they are strict about wanting the mortgage to be under $600 per month.

When they look around and there is a really lovely home they really like for $126,000. The $16K down payment they have is more than 12% down, but well below the 20% required to avoid paying PMI. Those PMI payments are going to be nearly $46 per month for the first 53 months (nearly 4.5 years).

After those payments are made, they will have to spend a few hundred dollars for a reappraisal on the property. If the property has retained value, the PMI can be removed.

If they took out a 30-year loan at 4% interest, their initial payments would be roughly $570.99 per month (not counting property tax and insurance). After 30 years they would own their home and would have paid a total of $81,485.62 in interest payments. The total loan payments (principal + interest) would have been $191,485.62. Add back in the $16,000 down for a total of $207,485.62 for a house they bought for $126,000.

$$

Now let's consider a different option. Imagine they find a really nice two-unit building in a nice part of the city for only $80,000. If they purchase this property, their $16,000 is exactly 20% down so they will not be hindered with paying PMI and will not have to pay hundreds of dollars for an additional appraisal after a few years.

This property also has the benefit of generating income through the second tenant (assuming the buyer lives in one unit).

If they took out a 30-year loan at 4% interest, their monthly payments would be roughly $305.55 per month (not counting property tax and insurance). If they took the loan to term, they would ultimately make $45,996.48 in interest payments. Their total payments to the bank (principal + interest) would have been $109,996.48. Adding the $16,000 down payment into the equation brings the total amount paid to $125,996.48 for the $80,000 property.

$$

Now let's consider a smarter scenario where the tenant is paying $500 per month for rent. The owners wanted to keep their personal monthly expenses at $600 for a mortgage. If they are disciplined enough, they could add the tenant's rent to the amount they were willing to spend and actually pay $1,100 per month on the mortgage. What happens to the mortgage with that large extra payment every month?

In this case, the building is paid off in 5.33 years with total interest at $7,262.74. Adding the principal and down payments back in bring the total cost to $87,262.74 for the $80,000 property.

Believe it or not, it gets much better than this. Remember the tenant's rent? Over the 64 months to pay off the building the tenant's rent would have totaled $32,000!

That means the owner paid, out of pocket, $54,262.74 for the $80,000 two-unit building. How does that sound?

Shall we make it even better? The mortgage will always stay the same, but rent can be raised. How often does the owner increase rent? That would accelerate this process and/or lower how much the owner paid for the building.

$$

Some of you are now thinking, "I don't want to live in a two-unit apartment building, even if I own it."

Fair enough. Let's get back to the original home the buyer really wanted.

After 6.5 years of owning their two-unit building, that other property comes on the market again, but the price is now higher. It is now listed at $138,000.

Since the fictitious owner is smart, they have been saving their tenant's rent and their own $600 per month since paying off their building 14 months earlier. This gives them $8,000 for down payment on the home they really wanted.

Let's assume they score another 30-year mortgage at 4%. The $8,000 down is not enough to avoid PMI. On this $130,000 mortgage, they will be paying $674.81 per month and be stuck with PMI payments for 89 months — nearly seven years!

After 30 years, they will have paid $236,251.19 (interest + principal + down payment). This might sound terrible at this point, but hold on a moment, there are factors not considered here.

This owner still has a tenant paying rent. They also now have a second apartment, the one they vacated, to rent. Assuming they had the nicer apartment, maybe they will get $700 per month for their unit and the original tenant's rent gets raised to $600. Assuming the owner still chips in $600 per month, that brings the potential mortgage payment to $1,900 per month.

If they are disciplined and can make those payments, then they will get rid of PMI in just 13 months!

If they maintain those payments, the house will be paid off in 6.5 years! The total PMI would have been $704.21 and total interest would have been $17,985.20. The total paid for the property would have been $156,689.41.

Let's not forget the amount the tenants paid toward this home. Both tenants' rent over those 78 months would have come to $101,400. That means the owner took over this $138,000 property with only spending $55,289.41!

$$

At this point, the owner would be 13 years into this process. They would be living in their preferred home (that is completely paid off) and own a second two-unit building that is still generating $1,300 per month of income *assuming rents are not raised*!

They would be living mortgage free with substantial passive income. Their two properties, originally valued at $218,000, cost them only $109,552.15 out-of-pocket.

This entire scenarios gets even more beautiful when you factor in that rent will most likely go up and that the property values will also continue to grow.

Now compare this scenario to them just buying the preferred home outright. At this point, they would be only 13 years into 30 years of payments and their total out-of-pocket expense would have been $207,485.62.

Which would you prefer: Owning your dream home for $207,485.62 or owning your dream home + a two-unit, income-generating property for $109,552.15?

Would you be willing to live in a two-unit apartment building for 6.5 years for this kind of return on investment?

Wait, *this still gets even better.* For comparison sake, the original preferred home would have taken 30 years to pay off. What does our second scenario look like 17 years after both properties were paid off in 13? Those additional 17 years of rent, assuming no rental increase, would have generated over $265,000 of income! The "investment" has truly become a source of income and the preferred home was basically free!

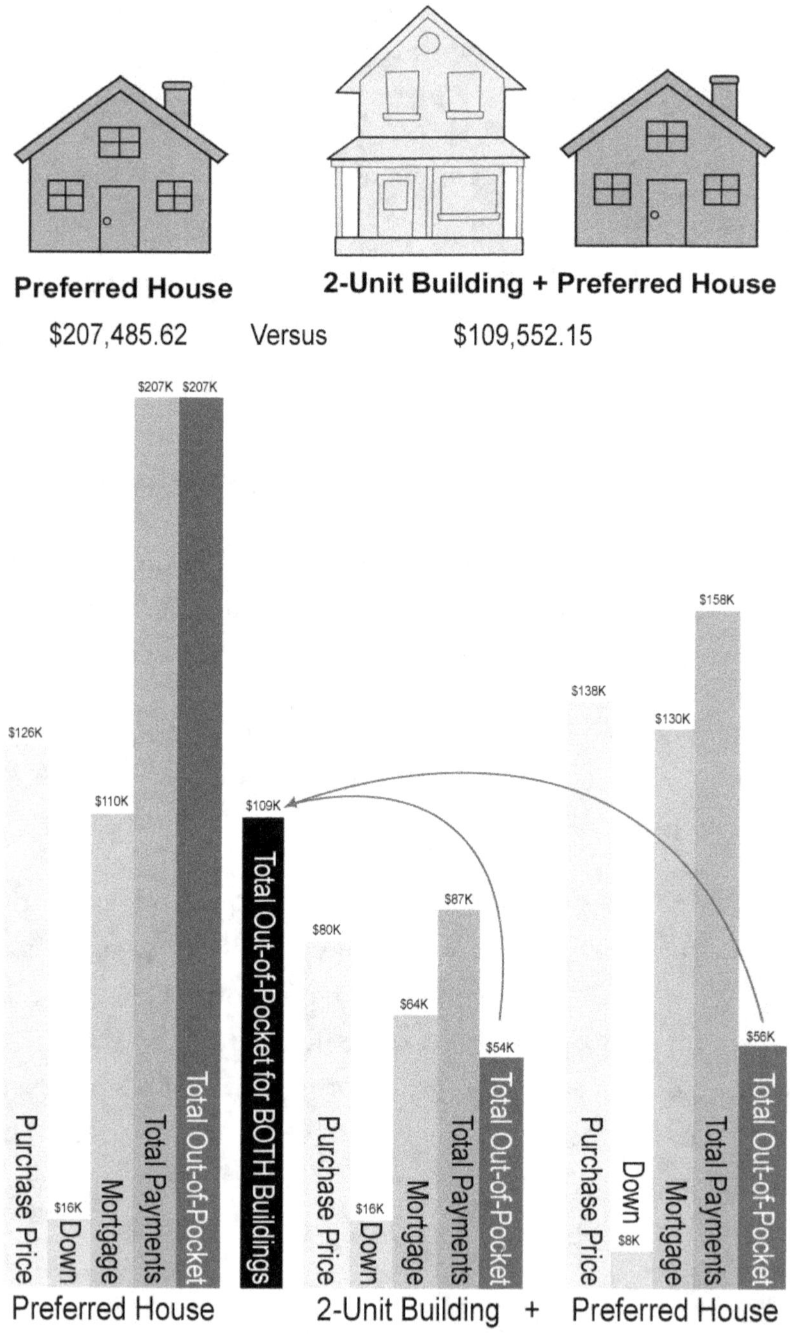

 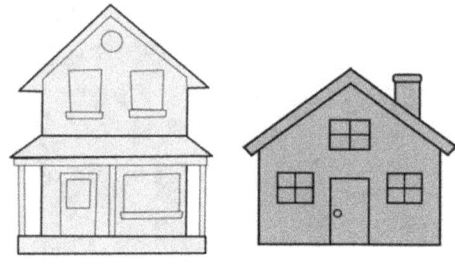

Preferred House   **2-Unit Building + Preferred House**

$207,485.62   Versus $109,552.15

Preferred House
- Purchase Price: $126K
- Down: $16K
- Mortgage: $110K
- Total Payments: $207K
- Total Out-of-Pocket: $207K

2-Unit Building
- Purchase Price: $80K
- Down: $16K
- Mortgage: $64K
- Total Payments: $87K
- Total Out-of-Pocket: $54K

Preferred House
- Purchase Price: $138K
- Down: $8K
- Mortgage: $130K
- Total Payments: $158K
- Total Out-of-Pocket: $56K

Total Out-of-Pocket for BOTH Buildings: $109K

Chapter 14

Comparing $50,000 Salaries

We are going to compare two individuals, Dave and Melissa who both just got new jobs earning a $50,000-per-year salary. They have been living in similar 2-bedroom apartments and driving 4-year-old Toyota Corollas. With their new-found income, they are going to make drastically different choices with their spending. Dave will buy what he wants, when he wants it. Melissa will demonstrate financial savvy. Let's see how their financial lives will compare over time

We'll assume they both have excellent credit and they both have saved $20,000.

A $50,000 salary will have a gross monthly income of $4,166.66 which sounds fantastic. As we all know, from that amount we need to subtract federal, state, and local income taxes. We will also have to take out deductions for health care and retirement contributions.

That might bring the actual net paycheck down to $2,880* each month (*this number is based on a previous position where I was making $50,652 while living in Pennsylvania).

$$

Dave is finally in a position to buy his new dream home at a very reasonable $175,000. The bank said he only needs 5% down so that will eat $8,750 out of his savings and his monthly payments will start out at $1,092.14. Since he only put down 5%, he will have to pay private mortgage insurance (PMI) for nearly eight years at nearly $70 per month. That will be roughly $6,442.11 in payments on insurance he will never use.

As Dave is driving to his new home, he passes the BMW dealership and sees that gorgeous new 5-series. He simply must have it.

The salesperson quickly talks him into a simple 3-year lease. He'll just need $5,000 at signing and payments will only be $529 per month for 36 months. The car insurance will run him $600 per year ($50 per month).

Dave is on top of the world with his brand-new home and sparkling new Bimmer. He is so excited to pull into his driveway. As he walks into his amazing new house, he immediately feels a sense of dread.

The house looks awkward with his "apartment" furniture spread out over the large rooms. Frankly, it looks silly in some rooms and sparse in others. How could he ever entertain guest like this?

He heads out to the furniture store. It does not take long for him to fall in love with a killer living room set, stylish dining room table with chairs, and talk about this new dreamy bedroom suite. Oh, and he can't forget to make up the guest bedroom really nice as well as he would want to impress his guests.

The furniture comes to $10,000 which is far above what he has left in savings. Thankfully the friendly salesperson tells him about their credit program. If he is approved, they can finance the furniture over three years at 12% interest with $2,000 down. Dave jumps at the chance for this amazing deal. They are so nice they are even going to deliver and set up the furniture for free!

His monthly payments will be $265.71. After three years he will have paid $1,565.72 in interest.

Dave is eager to call the local cable company to get that premium package he has seen advertised with 300 channels plus high-speed internet for only $125 per month.

His utilities will average $110 per month for electric, $50 for water and sewer, and $40 for trash. He has budgeted for $400 per month for groceries. With his commute from the suburbs, Dave will be spending $100 per month on gas.

Dave can't believe his new life — brand-new house, furniture and car. He has all of the best (and worst) TV channels. His total monthly expenses come to $2,786.85 which leaves him with only $93.15 of disposable income each month.

With such little leftover, Dave has to skimp on lunches, will not be able to add to his savings, and it he will not have money to entertain anytime soon.

As he still wants to go out from time to time, he starts relying on his credit card and dipping into savings. With his budget, he can afford a $25 per month minimum payment on the credit card.

He is stressed about money. Maybe he'll have to consider getting a roommate.

At least he still has $4,250 in savings.

$$

Let's see how Melissa is making out.

Melissa is also finally in a position to buy her dream home, but she also understands the importance of delayed gratification. She opted to buy the $80,000 two-unit apartment building discussed in the previous chapter. It is less than a mile from her new job and she is excited to get rid of the commute.

Melissa puts 20% ($16,000) down on the building and does not have to spend any money on PMI. Her monthly mortgage payment is $438.88.

She renews the lease for the downstairs tenant at $500 per month which more than covers her mortgage payment.

Melissa also happens by the BMW dealer and finds the new cars tempting, but thinks about the money lost driving a new car off the lot and the amount of time she will feel compelled cleaning the car. She is so close to work now, why bother?

She heads to the bicycle shop to purchase a slick new road bike for her short commute to work. There is a flashy new bike there for $1,600. As she is ready to buy it, she spies a slightly older model road bike on the used rack for $600. It seems very well maintained and in great shape. She chooses that one.

As a result, Melissa is only spending $40 per month on gas for her car. Since she is keeping her Toyota, Melissa is budgeting $200 per month for car repairs and her insurance is only $37.50 per month.

As she is moving from one apartment to another, she doesn't see a need for new furniture.

She signs up for high-speed internet at $75 per month, but does not get cable television.

Melissa's utilities are $55 per month for electric, $70 for water and sewer, and $40 for trash. With a smaller apartment, Melissa's electric is less than Dave's, but she is paying a bit more for water and sewer as she has a tenant to cover.

Like Dave, Melissa spends $400 per month on groceries.

Melissa's total monthly expenses come to $1,356.38 which leaves her with $1,523.62 of disposable income each month from her paycheck. She also has the $500 each month from rent which brings her disposable income to $2,023.62 each month.

Melissa is dedicated to rebuilding her savings and will put $300 per month back into that account. She also decides to start investing $200 per month in the stock market.

She knows the benefits of getting ahead on her mortgage payments so she will pay an additional $300 per month on the mortgage.

It's a big world and Melissa has dreamed of seeing Paris, London, Tokyo and more. She decides to also put $250 per month into a travel account.

The travel, savings, stocks, and extra mortgage payments come to $1,050 each month which still leaves Melissa with over $973 of disposable income.

Melissa enjoys going out with friends and she appreciates buying whatever she wants each day for lunch. A few times per month she takes road trips on weekends and enjoys a healthy dating life.

Monthly Expenses		
Expenses	Dave	Melissa
Mortgage	$1,092.14	$438.88
Car	$529.00	$200.00
Car Insurance	$50.00	$37.50
Furniture	$265.71	$0.00
Cable	$75.00	$0.00
Internet	$75.00	$75.00
Electric	$110.00	$55.00
Water	$25.00	$35.00
Sewer	$25.00	$35.00
Trash	$40.00	$40.00
Groceries	$400.00	$400.00
Gas	$100.00	$40.00
TOTAL:	$2,786.85	$1,356.38

Dave's monthly expenses take up almost his entire salary. He will be living paycheck to paycheck. Melissa's offers much more flexibility and significantly less stress.

Expenses Paid from Initial Savings		
Expenses	Dave	Melissa
Mortgage	$8,750.00	$16,000.00
Car	$5,000.00	$0.00
Furniture	$2,000.00	$0.00
Bicycle	$0.00	$600.00
TOTAL:	$15,750.00	$16,600.00

Dave used less of the initial $20,000 they had to start with, but he used his money to facilitate taking on more debt and, consequently, ominously more interest payments.

$$

Three years pass and it is time to check in on Dave and Melissa.

Dave wasn't able to keep up with Melissa's ability to go out with friends, enjoy lavishes lunches, or great weekend getaways. His social life did not totally suffer though as he relied on savings and credit cards to go out.

His savings is down to $2,000 and he is carrying a $3,200 credit card balance at 16% interest.

At this point, Dave has spent: $2,493.72 on PMI; $19,427.42 on mortgage interest, $1,565.72 in interest on the furniture, and $1,024 in credit card interest.

Dave has paid off his furniture and made the final lease payment on the BMW. Now he has to decide what to do about a car.

The dealer has offered to sell the car to Dave for $34,309. Its original price was $48,811 and he made $19,044 in lease payments. The idea that he would pay over $53,000 for a $48,000 car that is now used sounds awful to Dave. He also doesn't have $34,000 to buy it so he would have to take a car loan which would mean more interest payments.

With only $2,000 in savings, he doesn't have the finances to renew a lease on another BMW. Dave finds himself at the Toyota dealer trying to work out a lease on a more affordable car.

This feels like a backward step and just isn't going to sit well. He decides to go back to BMW and purchase his leased car. After all, his furniture is now paid off and he was used to paying that extra monthly fee so why not put that toward an $800 car payment?

Let's see how Melissa is doing.

Melissa's Toyota has been pretty reliable, but has needed $1,800 in repairs over the last three years. She had budgeted $200 per month for repairs, which over three years, was $7,200. The difference between what she put aside and what she actually paid was $5,400. She can now add that to her savings.

Melissa also has gotten into great shape riding her bicycle back and forth to work as often as the weather permits.

The extra $300 per month Melissa was adding to her mortgage payment drastically cut her interest payments. Over the last three years she only paid $6,824.35 in mortgage interest and the extra payments cut more than 19 years off of her 30-year mortgage!

Imagine paying off a 30 year mortgage in 11 years.

Melissa also was putting money back into savings at a rate of $300 per month. That added $10,800 back into her savings account.

Add this new savings and the money saved on car repairs to Melissa's remaining savings after the initial purchases three years ago and she now has a current savings balance of $19,600. She has almost completely replenished her savings account back to the $20,000 she had at the start.

Savings After 3 Years		
Savings	Dave	Melissa
Initial Amount	$4,250.00	$3,400.00
Saved car repairs		$5,400.00
Savings		$10,800.00
Dipped into savings	-$2,250.00	
TOTAL:	$2,000.00	$19,600.00

Melissa's careful financial planning has allowed her to nearly replenish the entire $20,000 savings she started with three years earlier. In fact, she is ahead of the game when you factor in her stocks. Meanwhile, Dave's savings has taken a huge hit He has not recovered even slightly. His financial picture is rather bleak.

Let's not forget that Melissa was also smart enough to start investing in stocks. She now has $7,200 invested in the stock market which is really increasing her net worth.

The $250 she put away each month has allowed her to take her dream vacation to Paris and London. She even had enough in that account for another weeklong vacation in the Caribbean.

Money Spent on Interest: 3 Years		
3-Year Interest	Dave	Melissa
Mortgage Interest	$19,427.42	$6,824.35
PMI	$2,493.72	$0.00
Furniture Interest	$1,565.72	$0.00
Credit Card Interest	$1,024.00	$0.00
TOTAL:	$24,510.86	$6,824.35

Dave's down payment did not allow him to avoid PMI. The size of his new home encouraged him to take on more debt for furniture, consequently leading him into a tight monthly situation that caused him to rely on credit cards and pay even more interest.

$$

Comparing the two situations, it is evident that Melissa has $19,600 in savings as opposed to Dave's $2,000. She also has $7,200 in stocks toward her retirement building and has managed to enjoy some sweet vacations.

Her credit is going terrific, net worth is growing, and she can start planning the next steps. It's not hard to imagine her now buying the same house Dave bought three years ago, but having the added assets of the two-unit rental property as more monthly income. Just like in the last chapter, when she buys her preferred house, the apartment she was in now becomes rental income.

Over time, she will far outpace Dave in both credit and net worth. She will always be more resourceful when life throws curve balls (car breaks down, hot water heater breaks, etc.).

Imagine how different life is for the two of them if they both are fired on the same day. Dave's world would come crashing down and spiral quickly out of control. Melissa would have resources and have several months' worth of backup cash.

Which situation would you choose? Which situation most resembles your current state of affairs?

If you are more like Dave, then you may be like millions of other people living paycheck to paycheck. Millions of people that do not understand how others seem to easily have money to save, much less invest.

Chapter 15

Money:
How to Spend It

Now that we talked about the importance of building net worth, improving credit scores, and increasing salaries all while saving oodles of money; there remains one question: On what to spend money?

This ultimately is a very personal question and one that I can't answer for you, but I can certainly share how my philosophy on what to buy has drastically changed over the last few years.

Before I explain how I value spending money now, let me begin with how I used to spend money.

$$

When I was 15 years old I got my first real job bussing tables in a fancy restaurant on weekends. The restaurant gave me a few bucks under the table and the servers threw some tips my way at the end of the night. It wasn't much, but it was a few dollars in my pocket and I was excited to be able to buy the stuff that interests a typical teenager (music, clothes, etc.).

Less than two years later I made it to the big leagues and started waiting tables myself. I was working four to five nights per week and I was literally rolling in dough. It was 1990, I was 17 years old, and I was clearing nearly $400 per week without any real bills.

With this influx of cash, I actually hit a "spending block," much like writer's block. I was quite literally not spending any money. Were there things I wanted to buy? Absolutely. So why didn't I shop?

I actually did shop, but the same thing happened every time. I would get my purchases, stand in line, and I would start to calculate how many tables I had to serve in order to make the purchase. Suddenly a $20 shirt was no longer *twenty dollars*. It was four or five tables.

I started valuing things on the literal work I had to do in order to generate the cash to buy it. This put me in a downward spiral of not buying anything at all. It was my 11th grade of high school and I was walking around with several hundred dollars in my wallet.

For a time, I actually got worried that I would lose the ability to spend. That is when I recalled seeing this incredible wristwatch a few years earlier at an upscale jewelry store at the mall.

I headed over to the mall and walked in to the store and there it was. It had a black leather band. The face was a deep green with a broad, muted-red vertical stripe. This was surrounded in gold with black Roman numerals in it.

Instead of the Roman numeral for "12," it had two Gs mirrored, facing each other. Just below that, on the face, in all capital letters it said "GUCCI" with tapered gold hands.

Hanging off the band was a price tag that I could clearly see indicating the price at $300.

The sales woman came over and asked if I needed help. I said that I wanted to see that watch. She seemed reluctant to show it to me and her nonverbal behavior indicated to me this was a judgement on my age.

I coolly pulled out my wallet and placed three individual one hundred dollar bills on the counter. I repeated my request to see the watch which she promptly produced for me.

I bought that watch and the spending flood gates opened.

A few weeks later I came back and about another Gucci watch for my mother and a few months after that I bought a second one for myself.

$$

The rebirth of my ability to shop, coupled with my new-found wealth, lead to a massive spending spree. I took a loan and bought a new car. I refurnished my entire bedroom and bought a whole new wardrobe.

I graduated high school, started college, and took up photography. I purchased all sorts of camera equipment, art books, art work, started stock piling IKEA furniture for the inevitable first apartment.

Soon thereafter, I got my first apartment and was buying all sorts of home décor, art work, and furniture.

I fell into a sports car addiction. I bought several cars, modified, raced, and, yes, wrecked them. I would replace them and start all over again.

My spending increased and increased. I wasn't just buying camera equipment — I was buying entire studio lighting setups and professional equipment to bolster my budding photography career.

My expenses on cars, photo equipment, furniture, and clothes far outpaced the cash flowing in from waiting tables. It started flowing out on car loans and personal loans. Unfortunately, it did not manage to outpace student loan borrowing. I'd borrow the max each semester just so I could keep buying more and more stuff. Stuff.

I was swimming in debt without a care in the world. After all, I was going to graduate college and get an amazing job with an incredible salary and pay it all back.

College graduation came. The amazing job did not.

Within a year of graduating, my world came to a crashing halt — literally. The latest sports car I had so much money invested in was crashed and was completely my fault. I had skimped on insurance so I was not going to get a dime for the car. I was stuck parting out what was left of it.

I was done.

I had no resources.

I had no credit.

I had no savings.

I was bankrupt and I hadn't yet turned 25.

$$

Over the next 15 years I would learn a lot about money, spending, and credit. I still shopped too much, but I did so within my limits.

I rebuilt my credit, bought a house, and managed to still play with a sports car but within the limits of cash — not debt.

In 2011, I separated from a long-term relationship and I drastically downsized my belongings. This is when I purchased my two-unit apartment building and moved out.

With a much smaller space, there was less need for me to keep buying stuff. Realistically, I didn't need anything else as I had bought so much "stuff."

At the end of 2015, I accepted a job in the Caribbean that was going to start in February of 2016. I had three months to significantly downsize even more as there as a limit to the moving expense allotted by my new employer. Furthermore, nearly all homes in St. Kitts are rented and sold furnished.

That said, I cleared out what felt like nearly everything.

Yet, I managed to still bring 1,500+ DVDs. I also brought my collection of ties (over 130) with custom-built tie rack and nearly 400 shirts with two commercial, retail clothing racks.

I still have too much stuff and I am certain that will be the last time I move those DVDs. They are practically obsolete.

$$

When I moved here, I was worried about the complete lack of readily available shopping in St. Kitts. It was part of my weekly routine to stop at ROSS, TJ Maxx, Marshall's, Staples, the malls, and many others.

I've grown to appreciate the lack of easy shopping. It was really punctuated the need to *not have stuff*.

It is a struggle to recall the last physical item I bought myself. I have lost the need and desire to own "things."

So what do I spend my money on?

My mother once said that before she buys something she asks herself one simple question, "How many times do I want to pick this item up and dust it?"

I like that question so I rule out many things that I am going to have to fret over cleaning.

As mentioned earlier, many objects ultimate demise is they get lost, stolen, or broken. That rules out purchasing things that I will be unhappy if that is their ending.

Also on the list of things to avoid buying are purchases that will become obsolete.

How much money did I waste in my youth on cassette tapes? CDs? DVDs? Walkmans (anyone remember those?) and other must-have-it-now electronics?

The purchases that I now most covet can't be lost, stolen or broken. No one can take them from me.

They are experiences.

My wife teases me that I use the word "experience" often. It's true. I would argue it's because I embrace life and what is life if not a steady stream of amazing experiences?

I enjoy travel, great food, museums, and shows. It would be a massive windfall to have all of the money I spent over the first 40 years on "stuff" returned to me. How many countries could I visit with that money? How long of a trip could I take? What amazing foods could I experience?

There's that word again — experience.

So, what do you spend your money on?

I certainly hope it's not $20,000 cell phones.

www.ingramcontent.com/pod-product-compliance
Lightning Source LLC
Chambersburg PA
CBHW052255220526
45471CB00001B/348